Singing in Your Sleep

SINGING IN YOUR SLEEP

The Personality You Will Need to Have a Career in Opera

Dan Montez

Whole Note Publishing

Singing in Your Sleep
The Personality You Will Need to Have a Career in Opera
By Dan Montez

Whole Note Publishing Edition
Copyright © 2011 by Dan Montez
All rights reserved.

Whole Note Publishing
service@danmontez.com
wholenote@optonline.net

ISBN print ed. 978-0-9801905-7-1

CONTENTS

To my wife, Melissa,
and her unwavering support
of this artist

Introduction

This is not a book about singing. At least, not really. In my previous book, *Singing for your Supper: What They Don't Teach in School about an Opera Career*, I said something that troubled a few people. I mentioned that becoming an opera singer requires a certain kind of personality and that most singers do not have the personality or the discipline it takes to achieve this goal. While the last book explained methods, techniques, and information generally ignored by institutions of higher learning, this book will lay out the personality that you will need to achieve your professional goals in classical singing. The methods described will not be easy and may even be disturbing.

Please don't misunderstand. I believe just about anybody can become an opera singer--a great one. However, few are willing to look beyond their techniques and skills and examine their personalities. In addition, few can see how their personalities affect their abilities to gain those skills in the first place. You may need to reevaluate your entire belief system and all of your behavior. You may be required to let go of your favorite personality traits that seem to define you as an individual. You may need to go visit a psychologist--a number of them.

The study of music isn't really about music at all. It's more about who you are, and what you will become as a person in the process. What you become will be much more valuable than what you achieve. Until you understand this, you cannot call yourself a serious artist. Your art will always be limited by who you are--your experiences, your personality, and your world view. Of course, many famous artists have different world views and personalities. Their differences are manifested in their art. However, they do have certain ways of thinking in common that allow them to express their art.

Unfortunately, many who want to be artists have no ability to express themselves fully. For some, it is a simple lack of colors on their artistic palettes. Others have a clear lack of technique. And still others have a lack of commitment to change, to accept criticism, and to grow. Once artists get past these basic problems, they can begin to create. Until that happens, their art is mere craftsmanship.

We will not get into a debate in this book about the definition of art beyond this. Debating the definition of art is a university exercise, mostly between professors who care more about originality than intention. These educators often worship the canvas and paints and disparage the artists who intend that their audience look for a meaning beneath the surface.

Hopefully, you are reading this book because you want to offer something of yourself that is edifying to the world, something beautiful, profound, and thoughtful. If so, you must understand that to share your unique dialogue with the world, you must get the world to pay attention first. That alone can create all kinds of problems.

One of these problems is the internal debate you will have between being "true to your art" and "giving the people what they want." There are days you will feel like a trained monkey and wonder why you are doing this at all. You will complain that the world doesn't really desire much in the way of art. It will seem that the general public simply wants the kitschy, shallow, or banal. When you offer something of real value, it is often rejected out of hand. The marketplace rewards the "pet rock" over that which requires growth, stretching, or any mental effort. They want you to be an entertainer, not really an artist.

So, why forge ahead? Does the world really need more artists? The world may not want more, but this is often because most people have not been exposed to true art. Even after they experience this exposure, they often do not understand the complexity of the language. Not understanding a language, be it foreign or symbolic, can put even the most intelligent people to sleep.

As a synthesis of arts, opera has the potential to reach people on many levels. It is one of the fastest growing art forms in the United States. For aspiring opera singers, there is a lot of room at the top of the profession. There are many singers in the middle of the profession. Either their personalities only bring them so far, or they realize that the sacrifices are far too great, and they stop at a level that allows them to be comfortable. Either way, the few who don't give up and are willing to do what it takes to create astonishing beauty have little competition and are always working.

The word astonishing is not used here lightly. Art should astonish. People rarely want to see a simple reflection of themselves, but rather something that is better than themselves. They want to be astounded and surprised at what humans can do. In addition, they want to be inspired to be better. How many times have you witnessed a work of art or walked out of a concert that made you feel as if you wanted to improve yourself, try harder, or achieve something great? Art that inspires this is rewarded.

Many people want to be singers. Schools and conservatories are full of wide-eyed young men and women who have been inspired by music and entered long programs of study, spending huge sums of money only to find out that they can't get jobs and don't have the required skills and knowledge to achieve their dreams. They hit walls, doors are slammed in their faces, they are subjected to cruel criticism, and they don't understand what they did wrong. Many of them have beautiful hearts, but very thin skin. They become damaged and jaded. They emotionally close themselves off as a protective measure.

Personalities need to be prepared to study in the arts at a professional level. Just about any personality can study the arts as a hobby. But the truth is these people barely scratch the surface of the discipline. They walk out of an institution of higher learning, having studied the arts, and believe they know a great deal about their chosen field of study. They do not. There is a vast difference between those who study art and those who are artists for a living. There is an even greater difference between those who have created a few interesting things with their knowledge and those who work and live at the top of their field.

Students often make it a pastime to sit in the halls and criticize those at the top of their profession. Learning to be critical is an important skill in the arts, but it can also keep one from respecting those from whom they can learn the most. The gap between students and professionals is great, and students often underestimate this distance. Budding opera singers are often shocked by the degree of perfection and detail required when they begin singing leads with larger opera companies. The examination, the artistic detail, and the profound introspection necessary at the top of the field can be overwhelming to the scholastic graduate, let alone the amateur or hobbyist. Schools are often ill-equipped to prepare singers for the onslaught of traditions, artistic demands, and professional requirements in the world of the virtuoso.

This book is a guide to the personality requirements of the professional performer. If you are willing to change what drives you and motivates you while developing your business and professional skills, then you will have a fruitful and joyful career. If you are ready to change internally as well as externally so that you can become the artist you want, this book will tell you exactly what you must do. Understand as you embark, this path is not an easy one. However, if you know anything about opera, you already knew that.

Chapter 1

Understanding Time

E very human being who achieves anything has the same twenty-four hours in a day. Some achieve great things with this time, and others whittle away at this precious gift by watching television or going to parties. Many simply sit around waiting for their bus to come.

How is it that some people seem to achieve so much more with the same amount of time? Are they simply more talented or educated? In most cases, they are not. What they do have is an understanding of time. There are many books on this subject, and you should read as many as you can. Understanding time is fundamental to great achievement.

As an artist, you have an uphill battle with this. This one issue may be the thing that keeps you from achieving greatness. Artists, by nature are fairly "right-brained," abstract, and random in their thinking. Their creative intellects are often disordered, and it is this very thing that draws many people into the arts.

However, successful artistic creation is not simply about creativity or originality, but requires order and a significant amount of "left-brained" thinking. If you are a musician, you may have all the musicality and emotion in the world, but if you can't perform an accurate scale or arpeggio, you will have no success.

Most scientists do not define genius by how much knowledge one possesses or how many neurons are in one's brain. Rather, the placement of neurons is more important. The ability of each hemisphere of the brain to communicate with the other seems key. Geniuses tend to have more synaptic connections between the hemispheres than most.

Dr. E. Glenn Schellenberg's famous study from 2006 found that those who study music significantly raise their IQs. Music requires both left and right-brained inter-communication. Translating the concrete into the abstract and back is a rare ability of not only artists, but all problem solvers.

Order is necessary for successful creation. Boundaries are necessary for successful creation. Yet artists everywhere struggle with this issue. Their drives and passions to create often interfere and conflict with their use of structure and organization. However, success requires that passions have boundaries. Your mind must be an house of order as well as a home of creation.

Time is the foundation of the order you must master. Not only must you understand it, but you must make it a life-long pursuit. Successful men and women are always tweaking their time, looking for balance. Time is the foundation and the scaffolding upon which you will build your mental mansions. Many people try to build their homes without the proper supports and structures and wonder why they end up with shacks. Some build something that seems rather substantial until it comes crumbling down around them because their foundations were built on mere passion and desire.

In order to understand time, you need to understand the

body and the mind and how they were set up to work. To do this, you need to understand habits. Developing habits is the first principle of achievement. Without them, you cannot build the foundation you want.

Understanding Habits

Your mind and your body are designed to work in one way—in increments. Most people don't obey the demands of this design. For example, too many people attend school to get a grade or a diploma. This often leads people to cram for tests or rapidly try to stuff information and abilities into their minds. However, life doesn't work that way.

For example, imagine that you have eight hours a month to exercise. What will give your body more benefits and create more results—exercising eight hours on one day a month or spreading that eight hours evenly over the month in fifteen minute increments? Your body is set up to work the second way. Your mind is no exception.

The productions we allow to be performed on the stage of our minds on a daily basis become who and what we are. Every minute we spend thinking about anything programs our mind, and subsequently, our behavior. It also works the other way. The actions we take on a daily basis create our long-term successes and failures. Both the mind and the body will consider periodic or crammed behavior an anomaly, not to be taken seriously.

This means that your thoughts and behaviors tell your subconscious what to attract. Your mind doesn't differentiate between what you want and what you don't want. It only knows what you spend your time with and assumes you want that. Then the mighty filter of the brain kicks into gear.

This filter is very effective. People who live near a set of train tracks can learn to filter out the sound of the passing train so they can sleep, yet if a pin drops in their baby's room, they immediately wake up. Our subconscious has a way of alerting us when it considers something to be important to us. Many people have had the experience of learning a new vocabulary word and then suddenly hearing it three times over the next week. This is not coincidence. It is not that the word wasn't being spoken all around them, but simply that their brains had filtered out something that was meaningless to them. In the same way the brain filters out these things, it also ignores ideas and information that do not correspond to our dominant thoughts and behaviors. It filters things out that do not correspond to our self-images. The subconscious will wake us up to opportunities that we have programmed ourselves to hear.

Again, our minds do not weigh our dominant thoughts as being desirable or undesirable when adding to this programming. This is also why we may attract bad things into our lives. Our mind thinks we want them because we spend too much daily energy thinking about them. This is why no one has the luxury of a negative thought. We cannot worry, fear, or even pray about negative things on a regular basis, or we will thoughtlessly lead ourselves down unwanted paths. The core of the matter is that we attract our fears. But we also attract our cultivated desires and reap the fruit of daily actions. So, if you pray, pray for what you want to become, not what you don't want to become.

In order to begin this programming process, we need to develop habits of both thought and behavior. A habit is not something that requires a great deal of concentration. It is not something we have to force ourselves to do every day. On the contrary, a habit is something we do without thinking about it-- something we do automatically. As a singer, you should not be interested in whether you can exhibit or perform a technique correctly while you are concentrating upon it. Rather, you need to be interested in those things you can do in your sleep, thoughtlessly.

You need to sing automatically. You need every aspect of your technique to be thoughtless. How can you become the character you are portraying on stage if you are still trying to remember to support, breathe, create a phrase, sing a pitch with the proper color, relax your tongue, lift your soft palate, cross your register break in the right place, or a hundred other things? How can any opera company decide to hire you if you are not sure and they are not sure what is going to come out of your mouth during every performance? In this business, surprises are unacceptable. All techniques must be over-mastered to a point of thoughtlessness. In other words, you must make them habits.

This does not only apply to physical behavior, but also to mental behavior. Most people live rather thoughtlessly and automatically already. However, the mental habits they have developed are far from desirable. Depending on how they were trained to think by their upbringing, this kind of "sleep walking" can lead people in many different directions. People could achieve a good measure of success if they all had good parents, good friends, good schools, and good experiences. But none of us have had perfect lives, perfect rearing, and perfect relationships. You may hear people say, "My parents did it, and I turned out okay." The fact is they did not turn out okay, and neither did we. To different degrees, we are all broken. The "sins have been passed down from the fathers" for many generations. Embrace that fact, and you have begun your journey correctly.

In order to change our mental habits, we need to leave the comfort zone of thoughtlessness and automatic thinking. This is just as painful as developing a new physical habit, like exercise, or eliminating one, like smoking. You must pay attention to your thoughts all day and even take notes. When you do, you may be surprised where your thoughts naturally gravitate. You might be astonished as to how much you put yourself down during the day or beat yourself up every time you make a mistake. You need to examine your self-talk during a voice lesson. You need to observe how you treat yourself after an audition that doesn't go well. Discover how easily you are frustrated. Find out how often you make decisions based on fear. Analyze your patience. Examine your feelings about those around you. How critical are you of other singers?

Everything you think makes you who you are. If you are highly critical of other singers during concerts or operas, you will naturally expect audiences exactly like you will attend your performances. Why would you want to sing for people like that? If you put yourself down on a regular basis, why wouldn't you try to live up to that low self-image? All of us are surrounded by negativity. We can choose to inhale this fatalism, or we can blow it out the window.

When you notice an undesirable thought, don't fight it. Remember that drawing attention to undesirable thoughts will simply attract them even more. In this way, we become what we fight. We strengthen what we battle. Prominent psychologist, Dr. John Fishbein expressed it well when he affirmed,

> *Attempting to battle or analyze undesirable thoughts is like trying to put out the fire by blowing on it: the fire burns brighter and the coals burn hotter.*
> *--Dr. John Fishbein, Emotional First Aid, p.25*

Instead, wave, say "hi", or say, "well, look at that" to your undesirable thoughts. Do not give them battle. Watch them pass by, then decide what you want to think about. Be ready with a desirable thought. If you have nothing with which to replace undesirable thoughts, your undesirable thoughts will take hold and dominate you. Ask yourself what you would like to be thinking about all day. What kind of person do you want to be?

Once you have an awareness of your mental behavior, it is time to work on habituating your physical behavior. Each person has a truckload of physical habits. These habits include how you walk, talk, stand, and hold expressions on your face. We may carry stress in various parts of our bodies. We have habits of how we deal with people, how we deal with problems, how we eat or exercise, and how we train our voices. Our mental states lead us to physical responses and behavior.

As we learn to sing, we may have to unravel years of bad habits by using new muscles and relaxing others. Then, it takes many more years to develop a whole new set of good habits.

Now here is the big secret about habits: Each individual habit doesn't take that much time! Many psychiatrists claim that it takes twenty-one days to either develop a good habit or get rid of a bad one. The process is simple. First, you can't miss a day, or you have to start all over. Second, you need to know it will be difficult for those three weeks. It may be hell. If you have ever started an exercise program or diet, you know that it can be quite horrible the first few weeks. But then, a habit begins to appear. Your behavior begins to be automatic and less psychologically painful. Third, you have to keep an eye out for old habits that will try to suck you back into familiar routines.

Daily habits do not take as much time as most people would believe. Just like the eight hours of spread out exercise in the example above, any skill or talent you would like to develop requires one thing: daily attention. If you want piano skills, language skills, or any other skill, do it every day. If you don't have two hours on a particular day to engage in that activity, then do it for ten minutes. Ten minutes are not only better than no minutes, but those ten minutes are vital to the mind/body programming discussed above. It must be every day. If you try to develop a skill on one day a week, it will take you at least ten times longer to develop the skill. When you do something daily, you tell your mind and body, even when you sleep, that you want that skill. This may sound a bit crazy, but synaptic connections are built in your sleep. Your subconscious works things out for you when your conscious mind is at rest. But it only works them out if you have proven to your body that you really want it. You can only do that by doing it daily.

Just like the exercise example, you will learn languages in fifteen minute daily increments at lightning speed as long as you do it every day. But if you try to cram that language in only once a week, it will take many additional years, and your skill will still be sub par. You can master all your skills in this way, and it will take up very little time. If you have time to brush your teeth, you have time to learn a new skill. And when you have mastered the skill, people will say, "Oh I wish I had been blessed with your talent," without realizing that in no time, they could have the same skill.

Few believe this. Most people believe that these skills take endless hours to develop or the luck of genetic inheritance. Endless hours are only necessary for those who haven't learned the secret of daily habits.

Waiting for the Bus

Developing habits is the foundation of understanding time. Once you understand that principle, you need to understand how to organize that time. After making notes about what you do with your thoughts on a daily basis, you need to make a graph or chart outlining what you do with your time. Again, you may be surprised just how much time you waste. If you can learn a language in fifteen minutes a day, then waiting for a bus is either a lost opportunity or a tremendous gift.

Successful people don't waste time. If you are out of work, what do you do with your time? You have been given a wonderful opportunity. Learn a new skill. Make yourself more valuable. Hire yourself. If you are an opera singer, you can learn an opera, then stage it, and perform it for yourself. Then put it on your resume as being in your repertory.

Carry language cards with you. Carry the words or music to an opera you are memorizing. Carry your laptop and write the book you've been wanting to write. There are many moments during the day that you are waiting in lines, waiting for the bus, waiting for meetings to start, or waiting for others to show up. Don't just sit around. Professional minds realize that there is only so much time in a day and that each minute is valuable. In addition, they realize that doing something every day for even a few minutes is like compound interest.

As you map out your day, you are creating a plan that is, by nature, unrealistic. You will encounter resistance to your plan each day. Unexpected things will happen, people will have their own agendas that will conflict with yours, and you may even realize that you would rather do something other than the thing you planned. No one can, nor should try to hold too tightly or religiously to any schedule. It will only fill your life with frustration. However, you must have that schedule anyway, even though it will generally not manifest itself in the way you expected. You will achieve more with the schedule than without it. When a plane takes off from an airport, the pilot files a flight plan. When headwinds come, the pilot doesn't turn around and come back home, but makes adjustments. You must do the same. Be flexible. If you have goals, you will always achieve more than you would have without them. Adapt as you go through the day.

As you deal with others throughout your day, realize that their time is precious to them as well. If you want to be successful, realize that your success requires the help and cooperation of others. Because of this, you need to respect their time. This means that you are on time or early to appointments. This means that you don't cancel appointments without an appropriate amount of lead time. If you do, then you offer to pay that person for their time, if appropriate. You come to appointments, meetings, or rehearsals utterly prepared so that you don't waste the time and money of others. Some opera companies have clauses in their contracts stating that you must be at least fifteen minutes early to rehearsals. These contracts stipulate that if you miss this early arrival more than a couple of times, you are fired. Opera is a meticulous business, and everyone's time is valuable. Creating a habit of respect for the time of others is fundamental to lifelong success.

Hitting a Wall

If you do not develop habits, you will eventually hit a wall. Some people grow up with just enough exposure to good singing that they have naturally developed some good singing habits. In addition, some people figure out how to create good sounds in unconventional, inefficient ways. But in the long run, all these singers hit a barrier in their progress. They may get hired to sing from time to time, but their careers will be erratic, sputter along, and finally die out.

There are many problems with the "natural" singer. They often come into university music departments and wow all of the professors and administrators with their singing technique. Unfortunately, these types rarely make it in the business. First, they never learned how to work hard for their skill. Second, because they didn't build their voices from scratch, they don't know exactly how their voices work. Because of this, when something goes wrong, and it always does, they don't know how to fix it. Third, because they learned incorrectly, like anyone who learns incorrectly, they will need to unravel what they have done and start over.

When students re-learn how to sing, they will probably sound worse for a while than they did before they started. Too many singing students are thrown off by this. They will come to a competent teacher or coach, having been singing for years-- even publicly-- and realize that lessons are making them sound worse. This happens because the teacher is forced to break down a house and rebuild on a new foundation. In order to build a mansion, the cherished shack, no matter how familiar, must come down. This takes a lot of courage and trust on the part of the student. If you get a bad teacher or coach, sometimes the shack must come down multiple times. All of this takes patience. There can be no shortcuts. You must go over the wall or through obstacles that present themselves and not around them.

Basic skills cannot be avoided in order to find a shortcut to success. There is no legitimate book entitled "How to Be a Great Singer in Ten Easy Lessons." There are no magic pills, no easy answers, and no quick fixes to vocal problems. Once you have a correct foundation and a set of proper habits, you will be able to progress as far as you want. Many singers try to save time by cutting corners and avoiding unpleasant aspects of their education. You may love to sing, for example, but hate rhythm skills. Every job in the world has undesirable elements. Some singers hate to memorize, translate, act, or deal with directors and conductors. Others have trouble with music theory, piano skills, or sight reading. Whatever your hang-up, learn to deal with it and overcome it. Stop whining. Don't ignore it. The things you most want to ignore and run away from are always the very things on which you need to focus. It is worth your time to develop these skills the hard way.

Wasting Time in School

Although you must not take shortcuts to a career, institutions of higher learning can try to influence you to do just the opposite. Schools can create useless curriculums that serve themselves rather than the students paying exorbitant tuitions. On the other hand, they can also offer valuable information to help you become a better overall musician. Your job is to separate the wheat from the chaff.

As discussed in the prequel to this book, *Singing for your Supper*, schools generally must serve the majority of students who will not become opera singers. These institutions are businesses and must be treated as such. Because of this, you do not need a diploma. You can get the pretty little piece of paper to hang on your wall if you wish, but you are likely to be a better student and learn more as a musician if you are not working for the diploma, but working, instead, for the knowledge and information. Most agents will take your educational achievements right off of your résumé as soon as you begin your relationship with them. They are not selling your diploma; they are selling your voice and experience singing opera.

So, how do you know if you are wasting time in school? You need to know which information is valuable and which is not. Schools assume you do not know and choose a curriculum for you. However, that suggested course of study does not always serve you because the same professors who make the decisions on curriculum may be the same teachers served by the decision. In other words, they choose classes that they teach or want to teach and not necessarily what the student body wants or needs. Money rules decisions, and since most students are not choosing to become opera singers, most classes may not serve your needs. Some institutions offer a Master of Arts rather than

Master of Music for this same reason. Universities require a well-rounded set of world knowledge including math, physics, history, politics, economics, etc.... Conservatories and other arts schools focus on performing and generally they are a better choice than universities if you know you are going to be a musician.

Either way, all of these institutions are beholden, unfortunately, to the mighty accreditation committees, panels, and adjudicators. To receive accreditation, an institution of higher learning needs a certain number of Doctors teaching in the music department. People who finish their doctorate degree, but have no singing experience in the professional world, will be hired to teach by schools rather than someone who has had twenty-five years singing at major opera houses, but do not have that doctorate. These businesses create doctorates to create more doctorates and so on. They are self-serving entities in large part. Actual skill for performing is not the priority at these schools, and they will not adequately educate you about the world of opera, even if they perform operas from time to time. Most singers, even with doctorates, come out of these systems with no idea how to write a resume or bio, get an agent or navigate a proper audition. They have had an inadequate number of required language classes, performance opportunities, or acting classes. Schools rarely require these things to the degree they are needed.

Don't jump through hoops, no matter how much the professors want you to. Calculate the amount you are paying at this institution compared to the number of units you are taking. A higher education is becoming almost absurdly expensive, and most of your money is going to administrative costs. If you take your hard-earned cash and pay experts to privately coach you in essential areas that relate to your opera career, you will find that you may more cheaply obtain a better education in less time.

So, what do you need to study, and what classes can you avoid? You can find an extended list with explanations in *Singing for your Supper.* You need to know the basics. Study piano intensively. Study theory, ear training, history, conducting, diction, opera literature, performance practice, and languages. When studying languages, study Italian, French and German until you are fluent. Don't take the required one semester at your school. You need to speak these languages. With today's competition, you will need extended acting classes. Study voice above all else. Spend your time in the practice room. It is more important than getting good grades. When you audition, your singing is what people will care about. They won't hire you based on your résumé. Grab every stage performing experience you can, including opera, oratorio, recitals and plays. The more you get up on stage, the better you will be.

What classes should you avoid? Ask yourself if the class will get you jobs as a singer. Avoid classes on bibliography techniques, form and analysis, orchestration, musicianship integration, twentieth century theory, and even art song literature and solfeggio. Don't write a thesis. Master of Music degrees usually don't require that, unlike many Master of Arts degrees and Doctorate degrees. It's your time and your money.

Some professors will be appalled at my suggestions. They will not only see it a threat to what they do for a living, but they will tell you that you will not know enough about music. But when is enough enough? You can continue learning forever. Musicologists love to do this. Does being a well-rounded musician make you a better performer? Absolutely. However, there is a difference between becoming a well-rounded performer, and being a walking encyclopedia. You need to be able to function in society, but you cannot be all things to all people. You can study forever and become the smartest musician in the world. But that won't get you on stage, and it won't get you a paid job.

Finally, stay away from choirs. Most institutions of higher learning are centered on choral programs and not opera programs. Many try to require your participation in their choirs as part of your major. The institution does this to serve the most people and serve their business. However, too many people are unaware of the fact that choral singing and classical singing have different goals and utilize different vocal techniques. The main goal of choirs is to "instrumentalize" the voice. While violins, for example, are trying to add vibrato and portamento to their playing to imitate the natural human voice, choirs are trying to take out these two things to create better pitch and harmonic definition. They don't support the true legato (portamento and in-between note singing), or the vibrato (the natural fluctuation in pitch), both of which promote vocal health. Choirs can produce great music, but they simply don't serve you as an opera singer. Spend your time and your money on things that will serve your career directly.

Again, these institutions are out there to feed themselves-- to suck you right back into the educational bubble and feed their business. They will even tell you that you need to do this to create something to "fall back on." These words are three of the most destructive in the English language.

If you create something to fall back on, that is exactly what you will do. It will be the focus of your time, and you will program your subconscious mind to unwittingly, or wittingly, attract this into your life. You are going to be a performer. Every minute you spend distracted from that goal leads you to greater distraction.

Even if you are afraid or feel compelled by a misguided sense of honor to create a fall back position, consider that following your own curriculum will make you a better linguist, a better actor, a better pianist, and above all, a better singer. This will make you more valuable to the marketplace than most college professors. If you did not make it as an opera singer, your skills as a private teacher will be worth more than they can pay you at any institution of higher learning. Working for yourself will always bring you more money, create bigger tax deductions, and give you more control over your time than working for a university or conservatory. There is no point on any level to create a safety net. That is a decision based on fear, and a decision sold to you by institutions to feed institutions.

Your time is all you have. How you spend it daily is what makes you what you are. Habits are the key to your success. Respect for your time and the time of others will establish the foundation you need to be the successful singer you want to be. Do not waste time waiting for busses, studying things you don't need, or getting sucked into the dreams of others at the expense of your own dreams. Although you shouldn't look for shortcuts around necessary skills, you should not waste your time jumping through hoops you don't need. Spend time getting organized, even if it is against your creative nature. Once you have this foundation, you are ready to move on to the other keys of your success, especially those discussed in the rest this book. When you do, you will see that they are all time-based. So make sure that you understand and embrace these principles of time before you move on.

Chapter 2

Practicing like a Professional

I f you want to be a professional singer, you need to learn that the majority of your time will not be spent performing. This is one of the biggest shocks to most budding vocalists. Endless hours will be spent preparing a concert or recital, and then in one hour--bang--the show is over. You are left wondering if that's really all there is. This is often the cause of "post-performance depression." What was the point of all this time? To hear applause for a minute or two? Your life will be spent practicing. It is all about the practice. If you are not happy with that, get out of the business now.

Practice is not about getting better. You may think it is, but ultimately you will rarely feel the satisfaction of self-improvement. As you learn more and improve your skills, you will be able to see even further--or see how bad you really are. As you improve, you will feel as if you are getting worse because your awareness will expand.

Too many people entering into the arts have an amorphous goal in their heads about the level they will have to achieve to

17

feel good about themselves. When they get to that level, they will be able to see much further. As a result, they may be even more dissatisfied with themselves and the level of their technique.

Practice doesn't end. If you get to the MET and you feel you have "arrived," your career is over. Many singers have sung at the MET once, and that was it.

You never arrive. You are either growing or regressing. There are no perfect singers and never will be.

Why Do We Practice?

Since we will never be perfect, we don't practice to be perfect. In addition, we don't take lessons and practice to make money. If you are reading this book you probably already sing better than Bruce Springsteen and Madonna. Yet look how much money they make. The public is easily pleased with inferior vocalists, so should we do something as hard as opera?

You know why you chose to sing opera. You probably felt that it was something you needed to do. You may have been driven to be the best kind of singer that you could be. Being an artist means much more than being a mere singer. There are two ways of looking at your life's work: either get a job to make money and try to learn to love it, or choose a profession you love and learn to make money at it. We study and train so we can live with ourselves.

Some people practice to get good enough to warrant attention. You may have entered into your life of practice to please or impress someone else. Perhaps you felt you needed to prove yourself to others or gain acceptance. On the other hand, you may have chosen this life to prove something to yourself. Ultimately, if you want happiness in your profession, a happiness that will affect your art positively, you will need to abandon your need to prove anything to anyone about how wonderful you are.

You are not on earth to get attention. You may get attention along the way, especially if you do great things with your life, but that cannot be what drives you, or you will have no peace in your life. In addition, you must understand that you can't separate the art from the artist. Who you are, everything that you are, will be manifest in what you create.

So, if not self-aggrandizement, what is the driving force of an artist? For those in the performing arts, where we are the focus on stage, this is a more difficult question. For example, a painter isn't the focus of his art. His painting gets all the attention. But when you get up on stage, people are looking at you. And yet, if you get up with the attitude of "look at wonderful me," your audience will perceive it a mile away. On the other hand, if you get up with self-deprecation, embarrassment, or any kind of stage fright, you have missed the point of your art as well. No one wants to witness an apologetic performance.

When we stand before the masses, we must neither be proud nor afraid. We are offering an imperfect gift; all gifts humans offer are imperfect. For a moment, we are connecting with our audience as fellow humans. If audience members reject our gifts or resist that connection, that is their choice. That possibility of rejection shouldn't keep you from offering. Your desire to give is about who you are, not about what anyone will accept. Of course, you want to offer the best gift you can, but you know it will never be perfect--and that is okay. What is not okay is hiding your imperfect gift or waiting to share what you have until it reaches some idealistic apex. Peace comes through the effort, imperfect as those efforts may be.

A professional is usually led by intention. We have something inside of us that we have to communicate, something we have to get out. For opera singers, we see singing as the most expressive and meaningful way to get that message out.

As we practice anything, be it karate or music, we will learn things about ourselves. Our personalities cannot be hidden from our practice. We will learn about our minds, our relationship to our bodies, our perceived purposes for existence, our patience, and our fears. Here is the bottom line: *What you learn while practicing will be more important than the actual skill you develop.*

Because private practice is so fundamental to what the artist does with the majority of his or her life, we will discuss it here. Again, the purpose of this book is to cover the personality you will need to be a successful opera singer. If you have a personality weakness in this area-- either with why you practice or how you practice--you need to clear that up now. You can change your motivations. Most people will choose not to, and that is why there is so much room at the top of the profession.

How Does the Professional Practice?

All professionals practice a bit differently, but they have more similarities than they have differences. The first thing to understand about practice is the principle discussed in chapter one of this book: you must respect and understand time. Professionals do not waste practice time. There is a difference between singing and practicing. Again, time management is key to your success as a performer.

You may have decided to become a singer because you heard someone sing, and it moved you. When you began to sing, it brought you a great deal of joy. When you begin to practice properly, it may seem counterintuitive. It may seem as if you are turning your back on the very reason you decided to do this for a living. But you must. You can spend your time singing beautiful songs, but that is self-indulgent. You will not improve, and you will severely limit your ability to connect to others and create beautiful art.

Many students enter college and begin the study of singing, only to quit once the hard work begins. They may have thought music was going to be an easy major in college, or that musicians sat around, like bohemians, singing all day in some kind of vocal utopia. The minute they start studying theory, ear training, or music history, they start thinking that they are not studying music any more. People say that they do not want to know how sausages are made, and there is good reason for that. In spite of the fact there are not unsavory items ground into the final product, many young musicians still don't want to know how a composition is put together. The more people study music, the more it seems to lose its magic and luster.

The situation is similar to the botanist who gets into his field because he likes the pretty flowers. Then he has to study the component parts of the cell and all of the other microscopic systems of the plant, and suddenly he isn't appreciating flowers as he used to. When he looks at a flower now, with his advanced knowledge, he sees so much more than the superficial beauty of the layman.

The more a musician breaks down his art into smaller components, the more beautiful it will be when he puts it back together. Simple beauty is anything but simple. There are those that create and those that appreciate. Those that create can appreciate, but they do so on a very different level. That level is not always intellectual. Those who create can choose when to turn off their critical minds and hear things through the ears of a novice. But, they can hear and understand much more as well.

As you learn to practice efficiently, you may feel as if you are being separated from the joy that first brought you into singing. Some musicians do allow their joy to be lost in this process. Since musicians are, by nature, professional critics, they can willingly be tempted into a negative mindset--only seeing the flaws in their art form. Again, you become what you focus on. Because meticulous criticism is necessary to create great art, a continuous flood of mental fault-finding can lead the artist to an unhappy life as an musician. There are many people like this out in the music world: cranky coaches, testy teachers, irritable accompanists, cantankerous conductors, and despondent directors. Many of them have forgotten why they wanted to be musicians. They have stopped creating any kind of art, but are going through the motions in their specific disciplines.

If you want to have a great and successful life as an artist, you need to keep a vision of why you are doing this every time you practice. Your practice should be filled with joy. You must love to break things down into the smallest components to be played with like a giant puzzle, that when put together, will inspire others, fill them with joy, and cause their jaws to drop floor-ward.

Practicing is like being a detective, searching for clues, finding the bad guy, and cleaning up the town. It is exciting and fulfilling. The pain, sadness, and challenges you face will create deep beauty in both yourself and the art you produce. So each time you practice, you must suffer a bit. It's a joyful kind of suffering. If you keep your joy in the process, your yoke will be easy and your burden light.

So what is it exactly that professionals do when they practice? How do they use their time? The following partial list may help you as you try to put yourself into the mind of the successful artist:

1. **Warm up.** Warm-ups are misunderstood. We warm our muscles up so we don't injure ourselves. Muscles are attached to your vocal cords, and, like other muscles in your body, need to be warm to avoid damage. But many believe that a singer cannot sing well without extended warm-ups. This is not true. People sing well because of superior technique. Some people use the warm-up as an opportunity to remind

themselves of techniques that are not yet automatic. But this is not warming up, it's just a technical reminder. Once your cords are warm, endless meaningless scales are unnecessary.

2. **Exercise.** After warming up, then we get to the real exercise. Those who are less skilled need more of this than the competent artist. However, even those who are skilled in their profession have new techniques they are trying to develop. This is the time they will work on those skills and develop new habits. In the early stages of voice training, vigorous exercise is necessary to build muscles--especially the diaphragm. After the strength exercises, then time should be spent with flexibility exercises, like coloratura technique. If you are a beginner, you may spend most of your time in this area. Singing actual songs has little importance to a beginner. Luciano Pavarotti, who studied voice daily from Ettore Campogalliani, wasn't allowed to sing any songs his first year--only exercise and practice. For most, that is the equivalent of taking seven years of voice lessons without singing a single song. That is one reason he became great (and why Mr. Campogalliani produced so many other famous top level singers like Freni, Tebaldi, Scotto and others). Some days you will only work on one note and one vowel for two hours until you feel you would pay yourself at a major opera house just to sing that note. You will work on that note for tone quality, vibrato speed, focus, pressure, volume, and beauty. It's all terribly exciting (say yes).

3. **Technical application to actual music.** This is the hardest of all and must be done slowly, especially by younger, less experienced singers. Again, this is not singing through songs. If you spent time singing one note during the exercise section, you may take two or

three notes from the song--with actual consonants--and spend your time on those. Work on how you move from one note to another, analyze your portamento, examine your dynamics and phrasing, decide how to deal with the consonants (are they liquid or plosive consonants, etc...), and check your support. If you are more advanced and have the basics down, begin with the hardest part of the song. Decide to make the hardest part the most exciting and best thing you do technically. Do not move to other elements of your song until you have mastered the most challenging parts. Next, if they are not the same parts as the challenging parts, work on the sections that are the most exciting for the audience. Work on them until you know they will make your audience gasp. Your goal is never to just be good, but to be astounding. Never forget that if you want to work. Next, begin going through the song elements:

    a.   **Rhythm and notes.** People can program robots to learn notes and rhythms. Music is about the choices that you make regarding the notes and the rhythms. It is not the notes and rhythms themselves. Many students feel proud of themselves because they get through a song without making rhythmic or pitch mistakes. When you enter the professional world and go to professional agent-represented auditions, you will notice that nearly everyone who auditions for opera companies and concert venues does not make note and rhythm mistakes. If you make no mistakes, then you have reached the bottom of the totem pole, not the top. Get these basics out of the way immediately so you can begin to make music. If you are still working on these things, you haven't even begun to be an artist.

b. **Registration check.** Vocal registration is common shop talk between singers that perform at serious opera houses. Unfortunately, it is hugely ignored in America because of the adherence by American schools to French and German methods of vocal technique and because of the dominance of choral programs at universities and colleges which know little about the subject. Vocal registration is to singing much like music theory is to composition. An advanced composer doesn't begin with music theory, but when something seems awry, the composer can go back to his theory to check his work and see if he has broken any basic rules. In the same way, a singer having problems with a song can go back and check register breaks to see if he or she is on the right side of the break in relationship to the pitch and vowel. In Rossini, this is even more vital, as coloratura, moving quickly, creates havoc for a singer who crosses breaks incorrectly and creates great vocal fatigue and strain, making it impossible to get through an opera.

c. **Diction.** The further you move up the ladder into bigger opera houses, the more you will be expected to sound like a native in the language in which you are singing. The larger opera houses will provide coaching by their linguistic staff, whose job it is to ensure you sound like that native. The small tweaks they make in accents are often so imperceptible (like differentiating between three types of closed "e"s in German) that it can be shocking to the new singer how meticulous this business can be. International Phonetic Alphabet (IPA) training is a must. Professionals go through their music in detail, so that they know exactly what sounds they are making at every moment.

d. **Integration with the Accompanist.** Too many singers are utterly oblivious of their accompanist. Not only do they not understand how to lead and control their accompanist during an audition, but they often have little awareness of the accompaniment to the songs they are singing. As a professional, you need to be aware of every single note and harmony played by your accompanist as if you were accompanying yourself. For this, you need to hear more than a melody in your head. You need the ability to process harmony. Professionals hear harmonies and understand what the composer was trying to say with the entire piece. Professionals are distinctly cognizant of how their voice part fits into a bigger picture. Too many singers act as if they are waiting for the accompanist to finish with their dawdling around with notes so they can get back to the real point of the presentation-- the singer. Wrong. Every note was written for a reason, and you must have awareness. Many professional singers are also pianists as well. They are well-rounded musicians who can accompany themselves.

e. **Phrasing and Dynamics.** So what is the purpose of phrasing and dynamics? The answers singers give to this question are often surprising. Too many singers say that the composer was trying to create variety--as if the composer were bored and needed to do something different. The composer was not bored. Every marking put in by a significant composer is accompanied by an important reason. Each composer knew what he or she was doing and what emotions he or she was trying to create. Always ask yourself, "Why is this dynamic marking here?" or "Why did he phrase the music this way?" You must come up with an answer before you even try to perform. In addition, singers need to understand that although dynamics are written in one spot on a page, that does not mean they are to sing that one dynamic across the notes in that section. The dynamic markings represent the median dynamic of the phrase. On top of that, no note should ever be held at one volume. All notes, either individually or collectively, are either going someplace dynamically or coming from someplace. That means all notes are either part of a larger crescendo or decrescendo. This is the foundation of all phrasing. Each phrase has a climax. Most of the time, that climax falls on the final downbeat of the phrase, but not always. Sometimes, there are waves, or double climaxes. We crescendo to that note, then decrescendo away from it. These phrases are clear, and the choices you make about your phrasing will often be one thing that sets you apart during an audition. You will base your decisions on what you perceive the composer is trying to express.

f. **Accents and Expression marks.** Like dynamics, composers insert accent marks and Italian musical terms for a reason. Make sure you know the reason and that you don't miss any markings. There are legato marks, portamento marks, tenuto marks, marcato marks, staccato marks, rallentandi, rubati, portamenti, and more. Having an eye for subtle detail is the mark of a true artist. Each mark conveys something the composer is trying to say.

g. **Performance Practice.** Performance practice is the study of how a composer expected his work to be performed in relationship to what was actually written on the page. Each composer expected different things, and each period had different conventions in performance known to those composers. Professionals regularly study performance practice throughout their lives. Classes in performance practice are not usually given until a singer is in graduate school, and then most of the operatic composers are not covered in the coursework. But that will never stop a professional. Too many singers and conductors today enter the opera world without adequate study as to how music was meant to be performed. It may be surprising to know that the most famous music publishers in the world have little idea what many of the markings meant in original manuscripts, and they continue to publish mistakes. For example, many of them insert fermatas into published versions of Mozart's operatic repertoire that were not fermatas at all, but rather signals of expected ornamentation and improvisation by the singer. Unless you had studied performance practice, you would not know this. What did Verdi or Handel expect the performer to do with a dotted rhythm? How did Puccini and Rossini expect their ornamental and melismatic figures to be performed? When do we perform an upper-note trill rather than an "on the note" trill? What is the difference between a grace note and an appoggiatura? When do we interpolate our own improvisation? Do we know what kind of a cadenza is appropriate to the musical era in which it was written? Vocal coaches and teachers who know what they are doing can help you with this in the beginning. But, ultimately, professionals become their own scholars and spend practice time getting this right.

h. **Interpretation.** Finally, after all your study into composer's intentions, there is still room for interpretation. In addition, each artist is unique and approaches a piece of music from a different angle than every other singer. In spite of the fact that you want to set yourself apart from other performers, you need to know what decisions you have the right to make about a piece of music. Some singers are very conservative and careful when making their own artistic decisions, while others are dangerous, risky, and still exciting. Interpretation often takes audacity. Some musicians will intelligently argue with a dead composer with the full belief that they would have been able to change that composer's mind regarding the composition. This is where debate gets furious. Performers will occasionally modify what is written, recompose, or rephrase a work to "improve" it or to adapt it to their musical strengths as a performer. The great pianist, Horowitz, is a prime example. Although most people look at a composer's work as sacrosanct, Horowitz would "fix" music he felt was "unpianistic" or "clumsy" in composition. Many musicians and critics were enraged. Many of Horowitz's alterations went beyond mere fixes and became "transcriptions," a word usually used to mean something is being set for different instruments. For Horowitz, it meant to change a piece completely until he believed it was better than that written by the composer. Interestingly, often it was. His gutsy moves paid off. Rachmaninoff, Prokofiev, and Poulenc regularly praised Horowitz's performances of their work - even when he took liberties with their scores. It is in interpretation that singers set themselves apart from the crowd and share their own unique vision of a composer's work. A good rule of thumb for the beginner is "First learn to keep and understand the rules before you dare to break them."

4. **End with a success.** Many performers find it useful and psychologically helpful to end their practice time doing something successfully. This can be important if you have spent time working on a technique and not

figured it out after a couple of hours. Ending your practice time with a failure can be detrimental to your future motivation. Even if you are not consistent with a particular skill, ending immediately after you do it correctly one time will not only lock that positive experience into mind and muscle memory, but will encourage you to practice again tomorrow.

Professionals are detail oriented to a degree that is shocking to the amateur or hobbyist, let alone the audiences that hear them perform. Again, the more you break music down and put it back together, the more beautiful and meaningful it will be. Joy is not really lost in this kind of dissection, it is only transformed into a different kind of joy.

Time must never be wasted in practice. Your time must be spent on the things you cannot do well and never wasted on what you know already. You cannot count mere singing as practice time. This takes a special, obsessive kind of personality. You must be committed to subtlety, precision, and exhaustive inspection. Then you must be able to see how the micro-scale fits into the bigger picture of the music you study. How are the small parts a piece of the larger whole? There can be no shortcuts. If you want to cut corners or achieve greatness without paying the price, then you need to change.

Practice is not something you do; it is something you are. Your daily focus will change you as a human being and an artist, and you will produce something that will fill your listeners with incredulity. That incredulity stems from the fact that it will seem superhuman to them. It will be superhuman because most humans are unwilling to pay the price for the kind of beauty you are going to produce. You will be an icon of human potential and inspire creativity, change, and vision in others. It's a good job to have.

Chapter 3

Mapping Out the Voice

You might guess that the personality of singers who practice as described in the previous chapter might also be just as meticulous in other areas of their singing and career advancement. You would be right. Singers at the top of their profession understand their voices in detail. They see their voices as a rich landscape that must be explored. Every step must be catalogued and organized as part of a daily expedition. Professional singers must know what is going to come out of their mouths at every performance. Hoping for good outcomes is never an option. There is too much money involved in opera for an opera house to take risks on singers who are not consistent and do not know their voices.

If you want to take away all doubt, then you must map out your voice in a number of areas. First, you must understand vocal registration. Then you must understand each vowel you

33

sing. You must understand your breath and the mechanisms of support. You must understand your high notes, the colors your voice can produce, and how to project your voice in an opera house. You must have an intimate understanding of your articulators and your phonators and how they relate to one another. If you don't have a meticulous, photographic memory, then you need to write this down.

Writing down the investigative work that you do on your voice will help you remember details about your discoveries: the results you get with each physical action, the sounds you create compared to your visualizations, and the successes you have when attempting new techniques. This record keeping will save you years of practice and years of lessons. It is like the good habit of keeping a personal journal so you can learn about your life and the progress of your character. We all learn from history, especially our own. We are indeed doomed to repeat mistakes when we cannot learn from our past. This is why we must write things down.

When you go to voice lessons or coachings, you should bring a piece of paper and anxiously await even the smallest ideas or suggestions that come from the mouth of the teacher or coach. Even bad coaches will offer at least one good idea during a session. Every correction they suggest should be logged and fixed by the following week. It is surprising how many singers will go to a teacher or coach without a tape recorder or even a pencil. A good coach will give you perhaps fifty to one hundred things to fix, and singers sometimes pretend that they can keep each and every one in their brains. Stop pretending. No one can do this, not even the best. The higher one goes in the profession, the more one notices pencils coming out of pockets because professionals cannot afford to make mistakes or forget even one important thing. If the coach has taken the time to mention anything, there is a good reason. You can take no chances, and again, your time is extremely valuable.

Mapping Out Your Support

Every singer should understand that support is the foundation of all other singing techniques. Breath management controls everything you do--singing with beautiful tone, singing high notes, expressing a phrase, or navigating register breaks. If you can't hold your breath back, and are dumping huge quantities of air to achieve your technical goals, then you need to rework your support.

So what is the rule of thumb for measuring a properly functioning support? Professional singers generally can hold any note between thirty seconds to one minute on a lungful of air. If you cannot hold a note at least thirty seconds, you shouldn't say that you completely understand support. Handel expected all of his singers to hold a note for at least eight measures. Those who have sung Handel, or even a number of Mozart arias, have seen long melismas on one word. Singers who do not understand support often take breaths in the middle of these long melismas, incredulous that they would be expected to sing these things in one breath. Singers at Handel's time indeed were expected to do this. If you can't do it in one breath, then don't sing the song in public until you can. Similarly, most composers also have expressed that cadenzas should also be executed in one breath. This rule goes for Mozart and Verdi as well. The endless inhalations of amateur artists is the stuff of singing stereotypes.

To understand your support problems, you need to know the problems you have in different areas of your voice. Draw a matrix or a use a spread sheet. Across the top, write the different vowels you will sing and down the side, write the different pitches that are in your vocal range. Next, start holding notes at the intersections of the vowels and pitches. See how long you can hold a note. You may notice some surprising things. First, you may notice than you can reach the thirty second mark on some vowels, but not others. This tells you that you may have problems with the way you produce certain vowels. You may also discover that you only have problems supporting in certain areas of your voice or only in certain registers. You may even discover that it is the combination of certain vowels and certain pitches that are causing your support issues. Discovery is why we map things out. You must know your voice in all of its imperfect glory. No one can grow without understanding, accepting, and embracing their flaws first. If we are in denial about our flaws, be they professional or personal, we cannot hope to change. We must always know who we are-- right now. Then we can change.

Mapping Out The Registers

Nothing is more debated among teachers than vocal registration. Many teachers are completely uneducated in this area. Richard Miller's books outlining the differences between the French, German, English and Italian vocal schools and how they relate to "functional efficiency" are basic texts for the aspiring pedagogue. Your degree may be in vocal performance, but every singer needs to be a pedagogue. If you can't teach or explain what you know, then you are basically flying by the seat of your pants. Learning how to articulate your technique in all areas of music is essential to achieving a consistent technique.

Singing for your Supper discusses vocal registration in more detail, so those details won't be rehashed here. However, it is important to note a debate exists so that you can combat ideas that are not based on facts. It is simply a physiological fact that there are registration events that occur at various pitches of the voice. How to deal with that fact is where the majority of these debates occur.

The French school is generally in denial with their "one voice" or "natural" method of vocal training. The German school admits the existence of these registration events, but doesn't want to talk about them or draw attention to them. In addition, the German school attempts to artificially darken and brighten the voice around register breaks so as to smoothly obscure any tonal changes. They also attempt to teach support through sympathetic muscle techniques like gluteal pressure or "squeezing the dime."* The Italian school neither tries to hide nor obfuscate the register breaks, but rather displays them in all their glory. In addition, the Italian method is more closely aligned to physiological facts and efficient vocal production than the other schools. Unfortunately, the majority of United States teachers and United States institutions of higher learning are held captive by German, French, and English vocal techniques.

Knowing exactly where to "put" or "place" notes (i.e. on what side of the breaks), is fundamental to long term vocal health and long term success in the business. Again, you must know your voice inside and out. To do this, you must map out your register breaks. In mapping out these breaks, many teachers and students believe that those breaks occur in the same place for every vowel that you sing. This is a mistake. The breaks associated with more closed vowels occur lower than those associated with more open vowels. The distance between the most closed vowels, like [i] or [u] are two whole steps apart from the completely open [ɑ]. Too many singers who accept the existence of register breaks stop short by not calculating this distance between vowels. This can also create many vocal problems if you choose, due to misinformation, to cross a break again and again in unnatural places.

Mapping out your breaks takes discipline. You need to find out where the breaks naturally occur. You do not want to create artificial assignments to these breaks. In the beginning, however,

*This may work for some, but try walking on stage

you may be off by a half a step or so. Learning to feel "why" your voice wants to cross in a particular place is something that takes intense, albeit subtle, mental focus. Sometimes crossing at one pitch instead of another doesn't feel terribly different. But in the long run, and during a long opera, it can make a difference.

To narrow down your choice of where they occur naturally, it is important to keep in mind the distances between breaks of different vowels. You must realize, for example, if you feel comfortable crossing a break on an [ɑ] vowel between F and G, then you should feel comfortable crossing the same break between E-flat and F on an [o] or [e] vowel and between D-flat and E-flat on an [i] or an [u] vowel. The distances between the vowels stay the same, even if your register breaks are different from those of other singers. This understanding can help you evaluate your own voice and help with the mapping process.

When you are finished mapping out your primary, secondary, and tertiary breaks, you can start using this information to check yourself. Learning to sing automatically means that you should not have to be thinking of this while you sing. You are not a robot and shouldn't sound like one. However, you need to have a mechanism to check yourself when something is not going well. You need to understand why you want to cross breaks in one place over another. After a season, you will feel it is second nature. But hard sections of a piece, especially a piece filled with melismas, need to be evaluated for vocal registration because of the sheer velocity at which you are crossing your breaks. You are less likely to stumble if you know the terrain.

Journal of High C's

One of the most important things you can do is keep a practice journal. Most students come to their lessons without a plan about how to remember anything that they learned from that lesson. Lessons and coachings are expensive, and most people cannot afford to be so foolhardy. Treat each lesson and coaching as a sacred rendezvous. If you return to your lessons time after time and are always being corrected for the same flaws, something is wrong. Either you do not keep a journal, or you do not record your lessons.

Your practice time is equally important. As you apply the details of your lessons to your daily practice, you will not have time to merely sing through songs at home. Make a decision now to fix your flaws permanently during the week you hear about them. While some flaws, like support, high notes, or vibrato, certainly will take more than a week, these things can be done quickly.

If you are a tenor, and you have the necessary goal of hitting easy high C's, then write about your daily efforts to hit that elusive note. Write everything.

1. Write down how you approached the note--from a lower note or by hitting it on the head, or by some kind of portamento or scoop.
2. Write down what you visualized as you tried to hit the note.
3. Write down what you felt emotionally.
4. Write down what you felt physically. Write down the muscles you remember using. Write down how much you remember using them. Write down the degree you used each muscle and how they worked jointly with other muscles. How did you use the diaphragm, laryngeal spacing, or soft palate?
5. Write down the muscles you did not use. Write down where you actively released tension. How did your tongue, your neck, your shoulders, or your hands feel?

6. Write down what you remember about the tone quality of the note.
7. Actively associate what you felt with what you heard.
8. If you recorded the effort, compare what you thought you heard with what you heard on the tape afterward.
9. If you didn't like what you heard, change one small thing and try again.
10. Write down the difference in action and result.
11. If you liked what you heard, try to replicate it. If you felt you were trying to do the same thing but got a different result, make a note of it. You did something different, but haven't developed enough sensitivity yet to differentiate subtleties in muscle use. Be patient. Take notes.
12. Understand the difference between what was weird or uncomfortable and what was painful. Feeling unnatural or weird doesn't mean you did something wrong. Pain means you did something wrong. Any time you try something new or buck lifelong habits, it will feel unnatural until the new behavior becomes a habit. Remember, this applies to character flaws as well.
13. Compare what you tried today with what you wrote in your journal yesterday.
14. Read and study previous journal entries.

As you write daily in this journal, you will create a habit of focusing on what you want. As you do this, your subconscious will take over, and your brain will begin working out your vocal problems for you. You will have mornings when you wake up and have an epiphany regarding your vocal technique. You will go to your practice room and notice that suddenly, things are working that were not working the day before. Not only will your muscles be getting stronger from your daily workouts, your mind will be solving the complex puzzles that have become your daily focuses as well. Your mind is happy to do this without you. Just create daily habits.

When you have mapped out the physical part of your voice and mapped out the dynamic, growing part of your voice, you are ready to continue. The kind of people who map out their voices are people who are not afraid of truth and the responsibility associated with that truth. It takes a special kind of personality. If you have a problem facing up to your flaws, weaknesses and imperfections, but feel you must create art, then set up a visit with your psychologist. Otherwise, you won't make it as a singer.

This profession is not for the faint of heart. If you can't fall on your face in front of others without feeling ashamed, apologetic, or humiliated, then start reading books on attitude and self-image. If you can't get up with a smile on your face every time you fall and jump back into the never-ending river of growth, then consider another profession. If, on the other hand, you know you must do this for a living, then overcome these character flaws now and stop complaining about how you can't help yourself. You can if you pay the price. You are not a victim. Now go buy your notebooks, pens, pencils, a tape recorder and come home and look in the mirror. If you don't like what you see, great! At least you know who you are. Now fix it.

Chapter 4

Acting in Your Sleep

One of the most egregious errors that schools make in handing out voice diplomas is in not requiring equal parts of training in both acting and singing. Any teacher or professional singer who tells you that opera is all about the music is simply wrong. Opera is a hybrid art form. Skills in acting are necessary, more today than any other time in history. Audiences simply will no longer put up with singers who cannot act. This issue may be the single reason that opera has been disparaged, ridiculed, stereotyped, and parodied--especially in the last century. If people think opera is just about the music, they can buy a recording.

As opera companies become monolithic, they tend to ignore the requirements of acting. This is, in part, because the opera houses become so huge that you can barely see the singer's face. In addition, they begin to substitute bad acting for ridiculously huge sets that dwarf the performer. In attending one of these performances, one may wonder if opera is about production design more than story. To the MET's credit, acting has, by necessity, improved as high definition live performances have been broadcast to theaters across the United States, offering a close-up view of performers not afforded in the actual theater at Lincoln Center.

Opera is theater. It is a story. Music, in both art song and opera, exists to serve the words--not vice versa. Good opera begins with a libretto, which, in turn, inspires a composer to present a musical perspective on those words. Composers who try to do the opposite by starting with the music usually fail. The same goes for those that try to translate operas into anything other than the original language that inspired the composer. The product often feels artificial and forced. Certainly, one can insert words into a good piece of music, but the music and the words feel disparate and unrelated.

In order for opera to succeed, the audience must forget that they are watching an opera. What this means is that there must be no "author intrusion." Author intrusion is something you feel when you are engulfed in a story while reading a book, and the author, suddenly, starts preaching, and you realize that you are reading a book. When you read a book, a good author makes you forget that you are reading. You completely enter the world of the narrative. If the author tries to preach, or does something technical to draw attention to himself, your immersion in the story can be shattered.

Opera is no different. Its magic can be destroyed in many more ways. The director can be so self-indulgent that his staging and concept have nothing to do with the story being told. The set can be a distraction rather than an implement to further the narrative. The conducting, lighting, and costumes can become an annoyance. But, above all, bad acting will break the magical "fourth wall" between the audience and the story more quickly than just about anything else. On the other hand, good acting can save a production and make the audience ignore all other distractions on stage. If singers are completely paired to their characters during a performance, it is next to impossible to break the spell they have over their audience.

Singing can indeed be expressive and dramatic on its own merits. However, a live recital or an opera requires that an audience sees the performer. If performers have a lack of connection to the characters they are trying to portray, the audience can see it, and the musical drama appears pasted on and artificial. In addition, a truly connected actor will sing with different dynamics and phrasing than those who cannot act. This is because the immediacy of their feelings will dictate that phrasing and dynamics. The phrases will not be inorganic or synthetic, but rather a natural outgrowth of the experiences of the character.

Schools that ignore acting as if it were an insignificant addition to the skill set of a singer have lost all sense of what opera is all about. Machines can perform notes and rhythms. Music is about what we do with those notes and rhythms. Interpretation is necessary in all musical disciplines. Musicians who have had acting classes understand the timing of intention in a way that makes them better musicians. This does not simply apply to opera. But opera requires acting skills and stagecraft. And since opera singers must be actors, they also require a certain kind of personality to act.

The Personality of the Actor

When one thinks of an actor, one often thinks of someone who is a little off-balance. Actors seem to be unaware of propriety and public etiquette, often speaking out of turn in emotional outbursts. They seem a bit crazy at times. They are professional liars. They spend their time learning to convince you that they are something that they are not.

In spite of this, actors are trying to portray more truth than anyone experiences in a normal conversation. They study and observe the behavior of people--their characters, personality traits, flaws, virtues, idiosyncrasies, and dynamic interactions with others. They learn to empathize with all types of people. They feel their sorrows and understand why they think the way they think.

This can give actors a bad reputation because they are often sympathetic to those whom the rest of society might disdain for unacceptable behavior. They are often acutely aware of the human condition, and as part of their training, have come to believe that people can change because they have monitored and studied the evolution of personality and character.

By adopting these evolving personalities on stage, actors become invisible, and they bring truth in the process. Two dimensional characters that are only good or bad draw attention to the actor. The audience realizes they are watching a show, which, from their point of view, has become unbelievable.

Actors are fearless. In order to completely immerse themselves in a character, they must overcome stage fright of all kinds. Without fearlessness, singers cannot do anything automatically. They cannot let go and allow themselves to become someone else. They cannot trust their vocal or acting technique.

Fear leads the singer to make all kinds of bad decisions. They try to force their technique, they become exhausted mentally, and they make everyone they work with miserable. Making decisions out of fear causes singers to attract the very thing they fear. Are you afraid you will not hit your high note? Then you won't. Are you afraid your acting will not look natural? It won't. Are you afraid your audience will hate you? They will.

Actors know that you must focus on what you want and be "in the moment" to be successful. People living in the guilt of the past or the fear of the future cannot possibly share beauty with others. Music is not innately beautiful--the interpreter can make it beautiful or disdainful. You cannot separate the art from the artist.

A fearful artist will hate his audience. He will wish they didn't exist. He will hate the idea that they may be there to judge him or criticize his precious art that he has worked so many hours to display. He will hate the fact they sold tickets to his performance because that just adds to the pressure. No one wants to watch a fearful actor.

The successful actor knows that he doesn't have to please anyone. He gives for the sake of giving. Fear and love cannot exist in the artist's heart at the same time. Shame and love cannot live together. One acts because he is an actor, and one sings because he is a singer. Singers give because it is in their nature to give. An actor who gives on stage is beloved by his audience. The audience can feel the love. The actor is emotionally naked on stage, and the audience is humbled by his willingness to share without holding anything back.

So, why the erratic behavior? When you spend your life trying to become sensitive to others and to feel things as deeply as you can, you begin to glimpse the world in a unique way. Your feelings ride on the surface. You don't put up walls to protect yourself from mental anguish like most people. Sometimes the actor has difficulty walking off stage and leaving the character behind when going home. Their fearlessness moves them to say what they think out loud, even when most would politely change the subject. An actor can begin caring so deeply for the plights of others that they will become almost inappropriately emotional about them. There are dangers in thinking like an actor.

However, what an actor does is so important to the growth of society that these things must be risked. The assertive personalities of actors are what makes them great at what they do and what brings change to the lives and characters of their audiences.

Now, as a singer, how do you feel about all of these personality traits? Can you imagine yourself being this way? Does it make you nervous? If so, you need to see the world in a new way. These traits are what separate successful opera singers from wannabe opera singers.

Many singers began studying music in school or singing in choirs. They were often treated as nothing more than instrumentalists along with the rest of the music department. Instrumentalists spend more hours in a practice room than vocalists, usually working up to six hours or more per day. Even if the singer is willing, vocal cords cannot take this kind of work. But this makes instrumentalists a different breed. They are often more introverted, separated from society, and staid. Singers, trained in this environment, frequently come out of school behaving the same way. When confronted with the emotional unpredictability of acting, they may resist.

Singers, on the other hand, must make personality changes in order to open up their acting skills. A university education has not prepared them for this. The few who seem to succeed at acting are those who have natural acting inclinations. Others must either fight their way through embarrassing failures or give up. Some believe you either "have it or you don't" when it comes to acting. It may seem this way. However, acting, like singing, can be studied and learned, and those who learn to reinvent themselves from the inside out often become the greatest actors.

The personality of an actor may scare you, but the payoff is huge. Part of the payoff comes as a direct result of charisma. You cannot underestimate the necessity of charisma in getting jobs, then getting those jobs again. Audiences pay big money for this kind of magnetism and a lot less for talent and technique. If you learn this now, you will save yourself a lot of heartache later. You must realize you are not getting jobs based on your talent alone. Most people reward charisma because they are basically afraid. They worship people who do not fear. Secretly, people wish they could be fearless and get up in front of others, regardless of whether they are accepted or not.

If you want this kind of charisma, you will need to get rid of your fears. Preparation gets rid of a certain amount of it, but it cannot combat your poor self-image. The feeling that you lack the worthiness to achieve great things will always get in your way despite the amount of hours you practice. Singers combat this in different ways, some healthy and some unhealthy. For example, some singers adopt the diva persona. It is a wall they hide behind that allows them to feel that the world owes them. It may get rid of fear, but it also gets rid of jobs. In general, companies will hire someone with whom they want to work for a month over the diva with the best technique. Those who master their fear by adjusting their love of self and love of others get more jobs and have a more peaceful life. On top of that, since one cannot separate the art from the artists, they are simply better artists.

What You Need Know About Acting

In order to act in your sleep, overcoming fear is not enough. Studying personalities is not enough. Like any other habit, acting must be part of your daily routine. You do not have time during a production or even a single aria to be thinking about what you want to feel at any given moment. Operas do not allow as much improvisation as straight acting. There are notes and rhythms that dictate exactly when you must feel a certain way at a certain time. In addition, music elongates your acting because it is slower than the spoken word.

If you have been college trained, focused mostly on your vocal technique, then there are a number of things you will have to learn about acting. Many of the basic skills are discussed in *Singing for Your Supper,* but you need to find a human being to work with you. No book alone can teach you how to act any more that a book alone can teach you how to sing. Go ahead and get your ideas from books, but ultimately, work them out with people who know. Books can also give you ideas about what to ask your acting coach. Here are twenty-five observed acting and stagecraft weaknesses that singers often have after they have finished their voice degrees:

1. Knowing how to walk on stage
2. Understanding and choosing subtext
3. Developing your character
4. Understanding your "singing field" as opposed to your "acting field"--cheating out
5. Knowing the order of acting: **thought** precedes **action** precedes **words**
6. Knowing how to listen to and interact with others on stage
7. Understanding the difference between the numerous internal and external focuses needed in a single aria
8. Understanding that your character is three-dimensional-- no one is all good or all bad
9. Knowing how to have your character evolve during a performance
10. Knowing how to do a basic double-take (for surprises or discoveries)
11. Understanding various ways to kiss on stage
12. Knowing how to fall

13. Knowing how to die in different circumstances (i.e. poison versus gunshot)
14. Knowing when to take risks or to improvise
15. Knowing how to time acting with the constraints of music
16. Knowing how to help others on stage--understanding your angles
17. Knowing how and when to cry versus when to hold back
18. Understanding comic timing and how to make people laugh
19. Understanding upstaging--its power and weakness
20. Knowing how and when to use your arms and hands
21. Knowing when to move and when to be still
22. Knowing how to adapt behavior to character and vice versa
23. Understanding how to create motivation from directed behavior
24. Knowing how to use your face, mouth, eyebrows, and eyes to create meaning, character, and subtext
25. Knowing how and when to breathe on stage--even when you're not singing

There are many more. Singers tend to leave school with a truckload of acting problems, and most graduates can't do any of the above twenty-five things. Some pick up a few by simply getting up on stage again and again. Performing opportunities will be rare for anyone who can't do these things first. This may sound a bit like a catch-22. It wouldn't be if schools were really in the business of creating professional opera singers. But most are not.

There are other ways to get this experience. The best is to hire a private dramatic coach to work your arias and audition repertoire. If you are still in school, then get involved in acting classes, in spite of your required curriculum. You can perform plays with a community theater (non-musical theater). When you do get opera jobs, be meticulous about asking for acting advice from your director and watch other singers for acting ideas. Write them down. Also, write down every single criticism or correction that a stage director gives to you. No matter how calmly they speak, stage directors don't usually tell you things that are unimportant. Professionals bring paper and a pen to rehearsal, eager to receive criticism that can be written down, no matter how trivial. To a professional, it is often the trivial things that are mentioned that have the most positive effect on the overall performance of the singer. True artists carry a feeling of gratitude for every idea they learn. Each job is a rare opportunity.

In the end, acting instinctively requires thoughtlessness. Just as correct singing should be involuntary, acting requires an ultimately instinctive behavior set. To do this, you must get up on stage again and again. You must adopt acting into your rehearsal routine. In the same way that you need to get to a point where you can sing well without thinking about your technique, you also need to be able to sing well while you are acting. They must be worked out together.

It is common for singers to work out the vocal technique of an aria, and then later try to shove the acting into the cracks of the prepared work. This treating of acting as an afterthought is a huge mistake on many fronts. First, singing requires muscle memory. When you memorize an aria, you not only memorize the notes, rhythms, and words, but you memorize each muscle that you used. The muscles react automatically with the music. Many singers, who think they are memorized, find themselves forgetting words as soon as a stage director starts having them move on stage. The muscles are connected to the words. When the stage director changed the use of the muscles, the words fly out the window. This is also why a singer who has learned an aria too soon, before their technique is ready, will find that inferior technique will stick with them, haunting them throughout their professional lives, every time they revisit that particular aria. Secondly, the acting will influence how you sing, how you interpret phrases, how you color particular words, where you breathe, and how you make decisions about dynamics and accents. Your spontaneity with acting will affect how you technically approach a song. If you haven't prepared yourself to handle the technique required for the character decisions you need to make, you will have technical problems during the opera.

Since muscle memory is so important, singing and acting need to be prepared together. You should try to act during your coaching sessions and voice lessons to see how it affects your singing. You may find during a voice lesson that it is a distraction from your work on vocal technique. This is a problem that plagues most singers--they can only consciously think about so many things at a time. But if you can only sing well with absolute concentration, then your wonderful singing will never bring you to a career. There will always be distractions. The big question is whether you can sing well and act well at the same time. After that, the bigger question is whether you can come to a staging rehearsal and have the director present you with a completely different vision of the character than the one you have worked out and respond without forgetting your music. It is sometimes a good idea not only to learn your music with your acting, but also learn it with different dramatic interpretations to prepare yourself for your work with a director. Either way, you will have no time to be thinking about vocal technique. This is another reason you must sing in your sleep.

Chapter 5

Accepting Criticism in Your Sleep

I rene Dalis, founder and General Director of Opera San José, once the highest paid mezzo-soprano in the world, is frequently known to tell singers that in the opera business, they need to have the skin of an elephant and the heart of a butterfly. Having a thick skin is hard enough, but maintaining a soft, sensitive heart while developing that thick skin is no small feat.

When a sensitive person is verbally abused and brutally treated, it is only natural for them to shut themselves off from feeling altogether. Why would people make themselves vulnerable again once they have been hurt? Psychologists make a good living answering this question. Through their doors come streams of patients who have been emotionally hurt by someone they trusted and who they never want to trust again. For many, emotional pain is greater than physical pain.

However, without the willingness to risk and experience emotional suffering, we have very little to share as artists. If we close ourselves off to the possibility of pain, our art will reflect this. We will also be unhappy. We must emotionally risk to be truly alive. We do not love because we expect something in return. There is no quid pro quo here. We love because we love. Period.

Good art is about contrast because all life is about contrast. Once we have opened ourselves up to the reality of pain, we are in a position to create better art. Joy cannot be understood without sorrow, pleasure without pain, light without darkness, or good without evil. They define each other. A graphic artist knows that putting yellow next to purple intensifies both the yellow and the purple more than if they were next to different colors. These complimentary colors reflect what we must do in all of the arts. If we portray only good on stage without any evil, the good will be vacuous. At the same time, if we display the dissonant without the consonant, neither has any meaning.

In his opera *Carmen*, Bizet clearly understood this concept. He introduces Michaela as a contrast not just to Carmen, but to the entire plot. Her goodness magnifies the mistaken decisions and the lifestyles of the other leading characters in the opera. But Bizet doesn't stop there. He continues to create contrast within each character. None of them is two-dimensional. They all have flaws and strengths, which reflect the truth of all humanity. They each struggle with their own natures at one time or another.

This brings us to our experience of the pain of criticism. As an artist, it is important to understand that when you do the courageous thing and reveal yourself to the public through your art, you are doing something that encourages people to criticize everything about you. When we share ourselves through art, we express a very intimate part of ourselves that fills most people with extraordinary fear. People care so much about what other people think that they feel the need to make excuses for not having the same degree of courage as you do. In other words, they may feel the need to criticize you for daring to do what they were afraid to do.

Remember, no one ever erected a statue to a critic. You can become like them, critical of every performance you attend, or you can learn to focus on what people do well and applaud those that truly give and share their art without fear. After you learn to love your audience, you will give regardless of their criticism or their acceptance of that gift.

Criticism exists in many forms. One is constructive criticism. Another is a simple attack or expression of disapproval. Sometimes the criticism simply takes on the role of an analysis, including the positive and the negative. And finally, another is the kind that gets written up in the paper by former sports writers who have no business writing about art. As an artist, you need to learn to deal with each one of these in a different way.

Whether or not criticism comes from solicited or unsolicited sources, too many beginning singers can't take criticism. Sometimes this is because they think they know more than they do. There is a lack of awareness, especially in college graduates, of how far they actually are from sounding and behaving like a professional singer. Pride is a huge impediment to receiving criticism, especially among those who most need it. If you have recently graduated with a voice degree, you need criticism--a lot of it. Your awareness of how little you know will take you far.

Constructive Criticism

The first time college graduates have a serious coaching from a non-college coach who works for an actual opera company, they will be tempted to run to another profession. They will be ripped apart, often corrected multiple times in every measure. The detail work can be shocking and discouraging to young singers. Most have no idea the degree of perfection that is required by the world's larger opera companies.

Constructive criticism can be your biggest blessing. Not everyone tries to offer ideas to resolve your problem after identifying it. Those that do at least want to help. The criticism may be valid or may be completely wrong. In addition, the advice on how to fix it may be equally right or wrong. So what do you do?

First, if you have heard this criticism before, it might be time to start paying attention. If you haven't heard it before, it may be valid, but you may want to get a second opinion. Ultimately, if you are intelligent, you can try things, and if they work, you can use them. If they don't, you can throw them away. Many teachers and singers are so afraid of creating vocal damage that they don't experiment. But, again, fear gets you nowhere. If you are smart, you won't be damaged for life. Relax.

Secondly, the criticism may be legitimate but the suggested remedy may be wrong. What you need to examine first is the person offering the solution. All too often, people with no business telling you how to fix the voice offer unsolicited ideas. Only voice teachers who have been professional singers themselves have any business giving you proposals to resolve your issue. Most coaches, by contrast, are experts at interpretation, language, and accompanying. They can tell you what they hear. For example, they can tell you when you sound tight or brittle, they can tell you if your vibrato is too fast or too slow. But they have no right nor knowledge to tell you how to fix your problem.

Unfortunately, vocal coaches, conductors, stage directors, general directors of opera companies, accompanists, conductors, agents and others who have worked in the opera business for many years feel that they know enough about the voice to teach. They do not. If they have not been singers themselves, working out the nuances of vocal technique in their own bodies, they should keep their suggestions to themselves. However, because many of these people are important to your career advancement and networking efforts, you can't tell them this. Instead, you need to smile and say, "Thank you, I'll give it a try."

If the criticism is legitimate, go to a teacher or even professional colleagues whom you trust for advice and ideas. There is nothing wrong with criticism of this sort. If it's true, use it; if not, throw it away. There is no need for middle ground here, no need for worry and angst. This isn't personal--it either helps you or it doesn't. Once you've decided, then let go.

Malicious Criticism

There are those out there, that, for whatever reason, only feel better about themselves when they are putting down the efforts of others. They offer criticism without invitation, and it is usually designed to make you feel worse about yourself. Some people are quite skilled at putting others down and can seem to speak intelligently about your particular field of endeavor. There are many self-proclaimed experts who define themselves by their myopic interest in all things opera. They attend every opera, they can name every famous opera singer over the past hundred years, and they can recite the Italian words to every famous opera ever written.

Then, there are colleagues, teachers, coaches, conductors, directors, choristers, stage managers, family members, friends, and insurance salesmen who will all, from time to time, decide that you have a big sign on your forehead that says, "Tell me what is wrong with me." Many of them feel that it is their duty to scrutinize everything about you--not just your singing--because you have "put yourself out there." You now belong to the public to be dealt with at their whims. To them, you no longer deserve either physical or emotional privacy.

When you face criticism from these people, you need to understand that it is all about them and not about you. Feel sorry for them. There is no need to get drawn into battles with them. Let it go. Sometimes people that you thought were your friends will come up to you and say, "Because I'm your friend, I feel you need to know what so and so is saying about you behind your back..." These people are not your friends. They have come to you because they didn't know how to respond to gossip and didn't have the guts to defend you. Or, they simply got sucked into gossiping about you and now feel guilty.

Gossip is the most malicious kind of criticism. It passes through groups of people, and it isn't designed to help people grow. Remember that if someone gossips to you about someone else, they are always gossiping about you to others.

One thing you should know, however, is that, like constructive criticism, malicious criticism might be correct. Because of this, you must embrace it the same way you do constructive criticism--without emotion. If it is valid, change. If not, throw it away. There is no need to stew about it. We get upset because we wonder if people are bad-mouthing us behind our backs and because we have allowed it to affect our self-images.

A singer has a more difficult time than other professional artists and athletes when dealing with criticism. Tennis players, after a fault, can look at their racquets; violinists can blame their violins or bows; pianists can hide behind their pianos. But singers are their own instruments. There is nothing to hide behind--it is just you. This is one reason singing is so personal. When you make a mistake, it's easy to see the voice as some outgrowth of your personality.

You cannot afford to see yourself this way when facing criticism. Instead, think of yourself as a car that needs repair work. People generally don't get emotional about that. When you work on your voice, it isn't personal. If you sing imperfectly, it doesn't mean you are a bad person. So why cry during your voice lesson? You are just fixing your car.

Analysis

As you move into the advanced levels of vocal training, you become your own best critic. Criticism becomes more analytical than personal. It becomes more of an issue of understanding how things work or don't work. It becomes more about which techniques you possess and which ones you don't. Good singers who want to get paid have an understanding of their own bag of tricks--their own set of special vocal skills that separates them from most other singers. They often get hired for those tricks. These may include your ability to sing clean coloratura, to float high notes, to decrescendo high notes, to move from falsetto to chest without a break, or to sing extraordinarily long phrases on a single breath. Whatever your special skills, you will, if you are smart, discover what they are and capitalize on them.

As you improve, analyze the voices and tricks of other great singers. Decide which tricks you want to adopt. You can work to develop all kinds of skills, even when everyone thinks you are wonderful already. When you begin singing in bigger opera houses, you won't be afraid to call these people and ask them how they do their tricks. They will take your call as a compliment. Even if you are not famous, you can often call on famous singers and offer to pay for a coaching or simply an interview. Most will be flattered. Don't be afraid of asking advice from great singers. Pavarotti used to regularly hear singers in his dressing room before a show. However, he did say that most of them simply needed to work on their support.

You will still have weaknesses in your voice. You will always have them. Growth doesn't stop. The minute you stop growing or think you have "arrived," your career is over. The more advanced you become, the more you will be tempted to believe you have nothing more to learn.

When you get to this point, something dangerous happens. You become surrounded by yes-men who will never give you a straight answer. Coaches, teachers, and others, will not dare to criticize your vocal flaws, because, if you don't agree with them, you will fire them or not use them any more. They cannot afford to lose your business--not simply because of the monetary loss, but the cachet of working with you. Don't think, if you are famous, that people won't use the fact that they work with you as a selling point, either directly or indirectly. You will give these people their value and pride. As a result, they will not risk their relationship with you by criticizing you.

This does you no good. As you improve, you will need people in your life that you can trust. These people must also know that you will not fire them because you have a disagreement about a criticism. You need to relish the criticism that you get at the upper-levels of singing because they won't come that often. Reward those in your inner circle that have the guts to criticize you about anything.

Newspaper and Blog Critics

Once you begin singing professionally, professional critics will begin writing reviews of your work. You may wake up in New York the day after a performance, only to have fourteen million people read about what an awful voice you have. Sometimes your friends will be so excited to see your name in a major paper that they will bring you the review regardless of its content. How will you deal with this kind of very public criticism? This may seem worse than simple gossip behind your back. A professional has made a value judgment on your work, and people will expect the critic to know what he is talking about. People will judge you without knowing you or even having heard you themselves.

How often have you checked the "tomatometer" at rottentomatoes.com to decide if you will go see a movie or not? How much credence do you give critics? Most people give them far too much credit. What do you do with this kind of criticism?

Here is a rule: If you believe the good reviews, you have to believe the bad reviews. Reviews are used by publicists and marketers. If you are selling yourself, you can use them if you wish. They are used to get people to performances; they don't get you jobs. If you send general directors of opera companies a copy of a review, they generally couldn't care less. They care more about how you perform during an audition than they care about your reviews or your resume. They don't care about your education, awards, or famous coaches. You must sing well.

When a critic lauds your singing, you can be glad that you made them happy, but don't get a big head and start thinking how wonderful you are. This doesn't do you any good and is annoying to others. If you put too much stock in the correctness of a critics' positive reviews, you will be devastated by their nasty reviews--which are sure to follow. You will feel the necessity to believe the negative comments they make about your voice because you trusted their positive comments. If you dismiss your negative reviews, you must also dismiss the positive things critics said about you.

Like any other kind of criticism, it may be valid. So, feel free to read your reviews, weigh and consider them, but do not blindly believe a thing they say. If the criticism is valid, change. If it is not, throw it away.

Since the criticism was so public, should you write a letter to the editor to complain if you disagree with it? Never. All publicity is good publicity. People will remember your name more than the negative things they said about you. Just like your friend who brought you the paper without realizing it was a bad review, anyone worthy to be reviewed is someone that most people hold in awe. This is why people start asking for autographs. They wish they could be criticized in a newspaper. The fact that you opened yourself up to public scrutiny is beyond most people's ability to comprehend. That is why you are rewarded by people--for having the guts to do what they are afraid to do.

****

By choosing to be a public performer, you have chosen a life of criticism. Because of this, you need to be emotionally secure if you are to have a happy life. Your self-image cannot be wrapped up in what other people think about you. Instead you must see criticism of any kind as a precious gift. It either gives you the ability to grow because of new, correct information, or, it gives you the opportunity to grow by learning how to deal with difficult people. If criticism is painful for you, you have some work to do--in fact, this book may be criticizing you for your inability to take criticism.

You need to accept criticism in your sleep. Its appearance should not be an emotional trial. Take it swiftly whether it was solicited or not. Make a mental note, then offer a genuine "thank you" to the person sharing the idea with you. Don't try to straighten anyone out, or tell anyone how inappropriate it is to offer you criticism. Don't argue and tell anyone why you do what you do. No one cares about your arguments. What matters is what you will do with the information. Change or throw it away.

Chapter 6

When to Begin Performing

M ost singers have little patience when it comes to starting their professional careers. They want to sing at the MET before they have shown that they will live the kind of life that a MET singer lives. If you were given a your first contract for a leading role at the MET tomorrow, would you change the way you practice or the way you study? If so, you're not only ill-prepared for such a contract, you won't be getting one soon. Job opportunities will come when you begin living the life of a professional first. Singers promise the sky "if" they get a job, but few are willing to work like an opera star right now without the job offer or the opportunity. Act like a professional today, and you will be a professional tomorrow. If you don't have the habits of a star today, you won't be one tomorrow.

This is yet another personality trait that keeps people from success. We do not pay a price for an opera career, we are that price--we live that price. This may be difficult for many to understand. Too many people see life as a measure of suffering. If you are religious, you may have been tempted to see life as a trial you must endure to achieve some reward later. However, what is the point of only temporarily changing your behavior if your heart wants something else in the end? You are not here to change your behavior, but rather change who you are. There is nothing more false than the idea that who you are is what you're stuck with. People spend endless amounts of money trying to discover "who they are" when who they are is malleable and changeable.

What you choose to do should not ultimately be a result of a "have to" and "ought to" mentality. You hear people rant about "needing" to do something or having an obligation, duty, or stewardship to live their lives in a certain way. But ultimately, this never leads to happiness, and it doesn't create great artists. What about what you "want?" If what you want isn't clear, or if you want more than one thing, then you have some work to do. Wants can be changed.

Are you a singer or are you just acting like one because of the circumstances? Do you do the things everyday that a true artist does, or do you only behave like an artist when you get a job? Certainly, changing your behavior can lead you to a change in your desires--especially if they are daily activities. However, things work better when the behavior flows from your desires. As you develop the habits described earlier in this book, your mind and desires will begin to adjust.

Another reason you may not be ready to perform is a lack of knowledge. Ninety-five percent of singers with a graduate degree are not ready to perform at a level that will lead them to full-time careers. Much of this is discussed and remedied by *Singing for your Supper*. However, you will need to have people surrounding you--coaches, conductors, and directors--who can tell you when you are ready. But remember, some of them will tell you what you want to hear so they can keep working with you.

You need harsh coaches. That doesn't mean they are disagreeable or condescending, but they will criticize your voice rather than clap their hands. You need to know when to move on from a teacher and begin going to a coach. You need to know when to move from one teacher to the next. Every teacher doesn't know everything. If a teacher tells you they know everything, run. All of them have weaknesses. Good ones will even tell you to see a particular person for a private coaching on a particular issue. If a teacher runs out of things to say, and they will, that doesn't necessarily mean you are ready to sing. Remember, you never arrive. There is always something more to learn.

So how do you know if you and your heart are ready for full-fledged opera performance? Begin by asking yourself some questions. Is your voice astounding to people? Have you already succeeded in memorizing an opera without being hired? How long did it take? Can you act while you sing without forgetting the words? When you get your first opera job, you do not want to embarrass yourself. Remember that your first obligation when hired to perform an opera is to get rehired. It is not to create good art. You will have many opportunities to do that along the way.

Different Levels of Opera Houses

Do not believe for a minute that the smaller opera houses do not matter. Again, opportunities will often come to sing in larger opera houses based on the level of professionalism you display at the smaller opera houses. You want people to hear you at these smaller houses and say, "Why isn't he singing at a bigger opera house?" At the same time, you do not want to act as if you think you ought to be singing at a larger opera house while you are singing at a smaller one. This means don't act like a diva. Companies can sense if you feel you are too good for them, or if you feel as if you are just jumping through some pitiful hoop until you get discovered by those who will truly appreciate your talent.

Every relationship is important in this business, no matter the level of opera house. You may find that you have some of your best artistic experiences in smaller opera houses rather than larger ones. The larger the house, the more unions and money start playing a role that actually can hurt the art. Although the players and singers may be better, there isn't as much time for discussion of character, role, interpretation, etc...Your conductor or colleagues may fly in the week of the performance and get shoved into staging that is pre-written for that stage.

Many singers who sing in "A" houses also periodically sing in "D" houses-- sometimes to try out roles and sometimes just because they love opera. Conductors and directors also move from house to house. And they all talk. This is another reason you need to behave like a consummate professional from the very beginning. Respect everyone you work with at all levels of opera houses--the costume designers, makeup and wig artists, accompanists, stage managers, chorus members, prop managers, and curtain-pullers. Don't do this just because they all talk--and they do--but because they deserve respect and because it is part of who you are. You want the reputation for having the kind of personality that everyone loves and wants to be around.

Although from time to time, you may feel that their artistic goals are different from yours, or that they are thwarting your ability to look good on stage or perform at the level of which you are capable, you need to know that they are trying to do the best they can too. Artistically, everyone is in a different place. Love will get you further than artistic integrity. If you help enough other people get what they want, you will eventually get what you want.

When you sing in a smaller opera house, particularly those that have less than a million dollar annual budget, you will find that they don't have many of the amenities of the larger houses. Come prepared to humbly do your own make-up and hair. They may ask if you have costume pieces of your own--especially if the production has a modern setting. They generally don't have professional vocal or linguistic coaches or accompanists, so, if you need them in order to learn your score, you will have to pay for this yourself (another reason you need to be a pianist yourself). Dressing rooms will generally be shared. You may be in with the chorus. The more you are gracious and offer to help out from time to time, the more likely it is that you will get rehired. If the company really likes you, they may even let you choose their repertoire for the following season to suit what you need on your résumé.

Smaller companies are the best place to build your résumé and experience. They are everywhere. One of the traits of professional singers is knowing the opera business. That means knowing where these companies are. There are many ways to get to know the names and locations of opera companies in the United States. You can subscribe to *Musical America*. They have a website and also publish a comprehensive catalogue annually. You can probably even borrow one from your own local small opera company. They get them for free every year. This catalogue lists all of the opera companies in the United States, with contact information and company size--"A," "B," "C,"or "D," depending on the size of the company's budget.

Professionals are always asking questions. They ask their colleagues where the local companies are and find out who conducts, directs, and hires at these companies. They find out how artists are treated; they ask about the audition process. They inquire about payment, if any, rehearsal periods, and repertoire. Professionals are always writing down information and building their reservoir of knowledge about the business.

In the beginning of your career, after you begin singing at opera companies that pay, you will receive offers from other companies that have conflicting or overlapping schedules. It will happen throughout your career. This is normal, and it is also a good sign. However, this is a pivotal moment for you. Your contract or agreement with an opera company is sacrosanct. Companies, especially the smaller ones, often make many of their most important financial decisions for their company based on your willingness to sing. They often advertise you as a singer-- letting people know that you are singing on a particular night. They sell tickets to people based on that fact, and unlike the MET, cannot afford to deal with a financial hit or demands for refunds. In addition, they usually rely on your need to build your résumé more than your need to be paid a handsome fee for your work. This is how they survive.

So, when you decide to back out of an agreement with a smaller opera company, you are not only inflicting great harm on it, but you are ruining your reputation as a singer. The new contract being offered may be better for your résumé. The opera may be at a bigger company and pay more. But a contract is a contract in this business, and you cannot afford the reputation as someone who will be faithful as long as "something better doesn't come along."

But what if the offer is so good that you feel you can't turn it down? You can speak to the company manager, inform him of the offer, but let him know that you are faithful to the company if he feels he cannot release you. Most times, he will release you. But, if he does not, know this: it is only because the company needs you and that losing you will cause damage. In addition, do not try to find them someone to take your place. Singers generally don't have the ability to compare themselves to their colleagues and know if they sing at the same level. If the person you recommend is worse, you will hurt the company, and they won't be happy with you. If they like the person better, they will hire them next time and not you. In any case, if they have to look elsewhere at the last minute, they will probably not hire you again.

You need to be grateful forever for the opportunity you received to build your repertoire at these smaller companies. It is good form to help them out throughout your career.

After each opera that you perform at these small companies, ask for feedback. You may feel that you are above this feedback and that the people running the small company do not know as much as you do about opera. You would be right in some respects, however, everyone in the business has had different life experiences and has something to offer that is useful. Whether good or bad, take it with a smile on your face. Ask what they think you could do to improve. Your willingness to listen sends them a message that makes them want to hire you again. But most of all, they will talk about you in glowing terms to other opera companies and people in the business.

As you continue through the various levels of career building, you will have to start asking yourself if the operatic offers will go on your résumé, will go in your pocket book, or will be favors to companies that have already helped you along your career path. If they don't serve any of these purposes, then you need to say no. In addition, you may have to make decisions between taking leading roles at some companies or taking smaller roles at others that will create more contacts and improve your network. For example, many singers attempt to build their experience by going into programs such as Merola in San Francisco, or the ones in Houston, Chicago, or the MET. Most of these programs let you carry spears for the big names in the business, but don't put lead roles on your résumé. However, much can be said for the amazing contacts and networking that goes on in these programs. You get to know many of the movers and shakers in the business and rub shoulders with big name singers. On the other hand, there are resident opera companies in the world like those who offer fest-contracts in Europe that pay young singers full-time wages to do leading roles. Opera San José in California is one of the few companies in the United States to do this.

Smaller companies prefer to use local singers. They cannot afford to fly you in or put you up someplace. So, you may want to move to a metropolitan area where there are many small companies and start making friends. In the beginning, work for free. After you get about ten leading operas on your résumé, it may be time to move on to getting an agent.

Agents and Networking

Getting an agent may try even the strongest personalities. Since this book is about the personality it will take to be an opera singer, you need to know now that to most agents, you are nothing but a commodity. Many will tell you as much. Accept it, embrace it, and get over their lack of empathy. This is a business arrangement to them, and if you don't make them money, then you are something that needs to be discarded. They will tell you this isn't personal. If you have never felt like a trained monkey before, you may start feeling this way now.

If you are a soprano, it will be even worse. Agents may actually make you pay a monthly stipend to represent you. The percentage you get will be less than that received by the men they represent. Again, it's business. Companies often don't want to hear sopranos because there are so many more of them then every other voice type. So if you are a soprano, you need to be significantly better than any man.

You need to know that, in general, agents will not work to get you hired. They will set up auditions, but they cannot and will not sell you as well as you would sell yourself. If they put their opinion out to opera companies that you are an extraordinary singer, and the companies do not like you, that opinion ruins their reputation for all the other singers that they represent. So, they will say to a company, "You might like this singer," in as apologetic a voice as they can muster. If the company doesn't like you, agents will say, "Yes, I've noticed those problems." They are a business.

Knowing that, understand that most of the jobs you will get in opera will be on your own. You will either get the job yourself through networking, or you will get it through your reputation.

So why use agents? Are they a necessary evil? Many musicians will say yes. Although many singers have careers without them, opera companies like agents for a couple of reasons. The companies don't have to face singers down and tell them they don't like their voices, tell them they are too fat, or tell them they don't like their personalities. It is also harder to say no to the face of a singer, especially a singer with a lot of self-confidence.

You can use this to your advantage, of course. Get artistic directors on the phone without an agent, turn on your charisma, charm, and sense of humor, and you will have a better chance of landing a job than through your agent.

Most of the jobs you will get will be through networking. If you don't like to network, you will fail in this business. It is all about networking. You are in business and you must sell yourself. If you have the hope that you can jump to the top of your profession and, like Pavarotti or Domingo, have people setting up gigs for you that allow you to simply show up and sing, you will be sadly disappointed. You may want to only be an artist, not a businessman. You cannot--especially at the beginning of your career. You must build your business for years before it will run itself. Even then, you will need to have business skills.

So, how do you network? You start by learning to be friends with people. You don't need to be best friends, or spend all your time with them, but you need to be a step beyond friendly. If you have a personality that doesn't like to write little notes, make phone calls, or go to parties, you need to make that change in your personality. Here is a list of your principal relationships that you will need to develop to be successful:

1. **Other singers and colleagues**--These are the people you work with the most. They are the ones who have the greatest ability to see your flaws as a human. Your personality will get and lose you more jobs than all of your vocal skills. People need to want to work with you. When you come to rehearsals, you need to ask people about their families. Find out about their days, their goals, and where they have been singing. If they are singers, tell them what you like about their voices. Be kind at rehearsals and help other singers look good on stage. You need to be genuinely interested in them. This is not a ploy. If you are self-centered and using this as a manipulative technique, you will be revealed, no matter how good you think your acting is. After a show, stay in touch, connect with them on Facebook or other social networking sites.

2. **Accompanists and coaches**--Pianists tend to have more contacts than anyone in the business without active networking. They work with everyone up and down the ladder. They can be a great resource because they know things that no one else knows. They know which opera companies are in town, and they know other singers, directors, conductors and other coaches. Treat these people with the utmost respect. Artistic Directors will often informally ask the opinions of their in-house

accompanists at an audition. You really want them to say nice things about you. Too many singers make the mistake of looking at accompanists as grunts whom they can order around. In reality, they are artists you need in your career. Be friendly, be kind, and be attentive to their advice. Thank them for their ideas.

3. **Conductors and directors**--In smaller opera companies, these can be the same people that run or administrate the companies. In larger companies, conductors and directors often come to auditions with company managers to deliberate on casting. Conductors and directors around the world connect with each other through a web that must not be underestimated. No matter how important you think your artistic integrity is to you, you must be a "yes man" to these people. If you can succeed in not only being an obedient subordinate to them, but also a friend, you have accomplished a great deal. Conductors and directors don't generally put up as many walls as those that manage opera companies. They may be your boss during rehearsals, but they may be open to closer friendships if you try. Like colleagues, ask them about their families or where they have been conducting or directing. Stay connected after rehearsals are over. Send regular updates on your performances and achievements. Don't be afraid to ask if they know of anything coming up for your voice type.

4. **Opera company managers**--Usually you will be hired by the Artistic Director of an opera company, not the General Director. Sometimes they are the same person, especially in smaller opera companies. At times, artistic administrators move from one opera house to another. You want to develop your strongest relationship with these managers. In addition to hiring power, they have more contacts with other opera company managers than

anyone else. However, they are the ones most likely to keep an arm's distance from any kind of personal friendship with artists. They know that they are running a business and do not want a friendship to get in the way of their need to do what is best for the company, which may include firing you. This is why they deal with agents most of the time. However, they are human, and many will speak and deal with you directly. Some administrators hate dealing with agents because agents can impede their ability to get things done. Your agent may ask the company for too much, causing the administrator to think that obnoxious requests are coming from you. In dealing with administrators, be careful using your agents. You want to develop a good relationship directly with the artistic administrator. Be sure to send notes, flowers, or whatever you can to show gratitude for your job. Never act as if they owe you anything, no matter how wonderful and famous you become. There are a hundred possible singers who can perform the role they are looking for and do a great job. You get chosen to do a particular role because of your personality and because of recommendations that come from others. Therefore, you need to be easy to work with while you are at the opera company. You also need to be easy to deal with when you negotiate your contracts. You may need to attract ticket sales. After you have been hired, let the company know if you have a local fan base. This will help a great deal in being rehired, so keep a database of all your fans. Build this database through social networking, church, and community service organizations.

5. **Wealthy people**--Money comes before art in most places, unfortunately. You cannot run opera companies without it, and you can't have a career without it. While

you have spent your life perfecting your artistic skills, many others have spent their lives focused on the acquisition of money. While you have the power to share your talent, many are happy to make art happen with their money. Opera cannot survive from ticket sales alone. It is not football. The free market doesn't support what is most valuable to any society. Because of this, an opera company requires donations and public support. Donations to non-profit opera companies are generally tax-deductible. Companies also receive monies from community and state arts councils and the National Endowment of the Arts. Although many of the governments of Europe directly run or support opera companies, as an individual artist, you need the wealthy to support your private career and the companies with which you sing. You will meet them after your operas, at opera previews or concerts, and at private fundraisers and parties. You need to go to these parties and shake as many hands as you can. Have your business card with you. When you do this at opera company events, you encourage the opera company to hire you in the future. You become a team player. If you create personal relationships with the wealthy, all kinds of magic can happen. Some may even offer to sponsor and payroll your early career. All you need to do is sing at their private parties from time to time or join them for dinner.

Networking is fundamental to your career. The more you embrace this, the more successful your career will be. You may have spent your life in a practice room and been reclusive. You need to change this aspect of your personality. If you don't, and you go to a party, people will know you don't want to be there and will read your insincerity. Get over yourself. The world doesn't revolve around you. Life is about others and your relationship to them. Your art is a gift that inspires others and involves others. Without your audiences, without your colleagues, and without your opera organizers, there is no opera. Networking is a form of gratitude--not merely a technique for getting lots of jobs.

So, are you ready to begin performing? If you think your voice is ready, you may find that there are other aspects of your personality or knowledge that are not. In spite of this, you can begin changing your personality along with your voice. You can learn to network, begin studies of agents and opera companies, and start planning how you are going to build your résumé and repertoire. Learn not only to act like an opera singer, but to be one.

Chapter 7

Offending in Your Sleep

M ost of the top tier artists who act like divas didn't start that way. Artists can change for the worse along the path. They start out right, but as they begin to get positive attention, they either start to overestimate their own value or underestimate the value of others.

In opera, the word diva generally has a double meaning. In one sense, it refers to the prima donna or leading lady in an opera. It also can mean you are a celebrity. When one envisions a diva, one often thinks of the exquisitely dressed super star stepping out of a limo on her way to a performance. On the other hand, the days of the singer's world are long past. Today is a director's or conductor's world, and the word diva has come to mean someone arrogant and spoiled.

Anyone who reads the paper is familiar with the stories surrounding famous divas who have fired from the MET for unbecoming and inappropriate behavior. The opera world won't put up with the diva, even at the highest levels anymore.

Most of the time, people who act like this are not aware of it. That's normal. Most of us are great at seeing the flaws and strengths of others before we can see ourselves clearly. So, for the sake of argument and a more thorough introspection of yourself, it is important that you, right now, stop and consider that perhaps you are a diva and just don't know it. Once you have opened yourself up to the possibility, you can start to pay attention to your behavior.

How to Become a Diva*

The secret techniques of becoming a diva have been carefully guarded and passed down from Monteverdi until they reached their fruition during the so-called Golden Age of Singing. They are shared here so you can, with careful study, ruin any chance you have of a serious operatic career.

1. **Refuse to talk to colleagues.** Remember, you are better than everyone that you sing with. You will not be treated with the respect you deserve until you demand that respect by separating yourself from others. You are distinct, and you sing "Quando men vo" better than anyone else.
2. **Take your positive traits and turn them into negative ones.** For example, take that tenacity that pushed you into the upper echelons of the opera program at Kalamazoo Community College and keep pushing. Never ask, demand what you want at all times.
3. **Throw tantrums if you don't get what you want.** Understand that whining is the key that will open the door to all of your dreams. People feel sorry for you. It

*The items in this list have been verified and witnessed as actual diva behavior by the author.

worked at home with Mom. Your plaintive tears will fill others with the desire to fix your problems and give you jobs because they know how pitiable your life is.

4. **Demand rides from opera companies and colleagues.** Others are so lucky to work with you that they should provide a way for you to get to your rehearsals and performances. Give them the opportunity to serve you, and they will learn their place. Don't forget to ride in the back seat.

5. **Complain about your costume--and be sure to yell.** Costume designers, makers, and others in charge of what you will wear on the stage rarely understand what makes you look your best. Tell your designers that you have worked with the last winner of Project Runway. They will be impressed. You know that your audience judges you by what you are wearing more than how you sing, and these underlings need to understand that. Rarely do they take their jobs seriously, so you must be on the look out for ways they are trying to sabotage your performance. They are, of course, jealous of your success.

6. **Tell makeup and wig people how to do their jobs.** Next to costume people, makeup people purposefully try to make your face look crooked, fat, or old. The wigs they want you to wear look like they have come from the Party Store. These proletarian drudges often need to be taught, so feel free to share your extensive knowledge that you have gleaned from waking up after hangovers.

7. **Don't look directors and conductors in the eye.** Remember, they are not your equals, and they are lucky to have you at rehearsals. When they speak to you, focus on your score. Who are they to tell you how to move, act, or sing on stage? You were hired because you already knew how to do these things correctly through your

correspondence course in the Alexander Technique.

8. **Ask the director where to stand.** When the director tries to tell you how to act, or discuss something called subtext, put up your hand and say, "Just tell me where to stand." That will shut him up. Directors just love to hear their own voices, and someone needs to put them in their places. No one really knows what a director does anyway, and you are tired of trying to explain it to people.

9. **Tell the conductor what tempi to take.** Come prepared to tell the conductor what tempi he needs to take at rehearsal. Most conductors don't know their ictus from a hole in the ground. Also, if you don't take charge of your fermatas, he will come up with ideas of his own, like cutting off your high notes before the audience is feverish and properly adrenalized.

10. **Refuse to try new things on stage.** Do not be tempted to listen to new ideas for your character or staging. There is only one way to do Violetta Valery, and it is the way you have done it the last seven times. If you get tricked into trying something new, refer back to number three above. You cannot maintain the respect you deserve and take risks like this. Remember, a courtesan is not a prostitute, and neither are you.

11. **Make sure the director understands your vision of the role.** It's the only one that counts. There is, of course, only one way to interpret every opera. This is not open to discussion.

12. **Don't talk to underlings.** Chorus people, techies, ushers, and other backstage crew have no business speaking to the polished artist. Keep your distance from them. You are not here to be friends with anyone--you are a professional. If someone backstage compliments your performance, they want something from you. Make sure you don't give it to them.

13. **Blame the stage manager or prop master when things go wrong near you.** Never take responsibility for mistakes. People must never suspect that you make them or you will lose their respect. Learn to deflect attention. Companies have stage managers and other underlings to take responsibility for anything that goes wrong. Use them!

14. **When criticized, defend yourself promptly.** Never consider criticism. If you do, you will be admitting that you are human, which, of course, you are not. Constructive criticism is something one gives to the people who build the set.

15. **Make sure everyone knows how lucky they are to have you near them.** Many need to be reminded of this. Inform them of your experience and expertise by handing them your bio or a recent demo tape. Tell them you hope they can pick something up from your vast repertoire of techniques.

16. **Tell the opera company that you want a different dressing room.** You may be fine with the one you have, but it is important to establish who is in charge.

17. **If someone else has the dressing room you want, throw her belongings out in the hall when she is gone and move your things in.** This will give you the reputation that you want and put your colleagues in their places. No diva should have to put up with a lack of respect this way. The opera is held together by Musetta and not Mimi.

18. **Tell your counterpart where to stand on stage so you look great.** Remember, you must never, never be an ensemble performer. You are not part of any team. You are the reason the company has sold so many dress circle tickets. The tenor is there to support you during a performance. If you must, grab his shoulders, move him

to where you want, and tersely exclaim, "Stand here!"
He'll get the idea.

19. **Make sure everyone knows where you have just sung, where you are singing next, and what awards you have won.** Unfortunately, many people do not realize who they have the privilege of working with. Be willing to help them out. Some awards fit nicely around your neck and can be worn.

20. **Tell everyone that no one understands you.** If colleagues, directors, conductors and other people associated with the production don't agree with you about even the minutest detail, understand that everyone doesn't think on your level. If they understood you, they would, of course, agree with you. Most people just aren't educated and can't think as clearly as you can. This is a cross you will have to bear especially when trying to explain the complexities of characters like Nadir, Beppe, or Nemorino.

21. **If you ever rub shoulders with famous people, let your colleagues know.** It is their privilege to know you are on a first name basis with Placido and Renée. This can establish their place in relationship to yours. If your colleagues claim to know anyone famous, they are lying.

22. **Try to show up late for rehearsals.** Remember that divas always deserve a grand entrance. Always be prepared with good reason like, "my limo driver was late," "I misplaced my tiara," or "I lost my rehearsal schedule."

23. **Try to find out what everyone else is getting paid.** You need to be sure that you are getting the most. If someone is getting less, don't say anything. But all negotiations with the opera company should be based on what it is paying others. You must always get the most.

24. **Tell everyone why you understand the "composer's**

intentions." Make sure you use these words as often as possible so everyone knows that you have a direct pipeline to the dead. You are the reincarnation of Verdi, and your friend at the Psychic Friends Network has expressed Puccini's wishes to you directly.

25. **Make sure every conversation turns back to you.** After all, your life is more exciting than everyone else's. You can redirect these conversations by expressing your opinion on any subject matter. For example, if others are discussing the benefits of breathing steam, then express how it has affected you throughout your life. The pain of others is really about your pain, and other people's successes are really yours. Others are blessed to hear your perspectives.

26. **Prepare your music on your own time schedule.** A rehearsal schedule represents constraints created by small minds. As long as you are ready by opening night, no one should complain. If others don't like it, they can easily be replaced. Refer back to number three for guidance.

27. **Hang pictures of yourself throughout your house, preferably pictures of you in costume.** Have a wall-sized portrait done and put it in your living room. Your friends and family, lucky enough to be in your home, need to remember just who you are and what you have accomplished. A strategically placed portrait can do the job.

28. **Wear diva clothes.** Understand the wardrobe of a diva. Never be caught in public in jeans or t-shirts. You are an icon and example to the world. Respect comes from what you wear, not who you are. Well-placed Prada will separate you from the masses and reinforce their place of inferiority.

29. **Eat only at restaurants where you are recognized.**

Make sure they have a posted and signed 8x10 headshot.
When someone doesn't recognize you, just point at the
black and white on the wall. Make sure you have a
special table reserved after the opera for you and those
lucky enough to dine with you.

30. **Carry around metallic pens at all times in case
people want your headshot autographed.** You never
know. If people are too shy to ask you for your
autograph, help them by offering. They will thank you
later.

31. **If you have children, understand that they are a
representation of you.** Dress them appropriately and
then ignore them. Let nannies raise them and make sure
your offspring understand how lucky they are to have you
as a mother. Study the wonderful parenting techniques
exemplified by Faye Dunaway in the movie *Mommy
Dearest.*

32. **Create tension backstage to create better drama
onstage.** When you do this, your audience will be
astounded as to how realistic and energized your
character is onstage. Your Cio Cio San will never be the
same. It works best if you get people, especially
volunteers, to cry. If they don't like it, they can get a real
job.

33. **Know the home phone number of the general
director of the opera company.** Never go through
company slaves. Always go directly to the boss. Don't
worry if the general director seems busy when the stage
manager fails to bring water to rehearsal, when you need
your prop letter to look more like parchment, or when
the accompanist refuses to compliment you after
rehearsal. For someone of your stature, even the smallest
of issues must go through the company manager.

34. **Ask for more than your share of complimentary**

tickets. Your entourage shouldn't have to pay. The smaller the company is, the more willing they should be to offer the tickets because their house will not sell out. Remind them of this if they hesitate.

35. **To establish your dominance, create a power play that you know you can win.** There are many ways to do this. Ask for pay raises, request extra comp tickets, or demand to have that aria cut that you have never liked. Sometimes, the best time to do this is right before the opera begins, when it is too late to call your cover. If the company says no to any demand, refuse to go on stage.

36. **Believe that what you do is more important than what anyone else does.** People that have chosen other career paths have given up on life. Be sure, in the most general terms, to denigrate others for their life choices. You have worked harder, longer, and more intelligently than anyone else in any other profession.

There are, of course, many other traits of a diva. But this should give you a basic picture of the kind of a person you can become over time. Many singers are humble in the beginning. But slowly, almost unnoticeably, the diva mentality can begin to take over after the singer begins to receive positive attention from the public.

People don't plan to become divas, but they aren't usually aware after they have changed. Obviously, it is difficult to have a meaningful and successful career with these attitudes. What do you do to make sure that you aren't falling prey to this kind of negative personality change?

How to Keep your Personality from Getting Worse

Of all personality traits, pride is the most destructive to the career of a singer. Because of this, you need to destroy even the suggestion of pride when you are trying to build relationships. Here is a more serious list of ways to protect yourself from the temptations of this destructive trait as you climb the ladder of an opera career:

1. **When you go to an opera company, decide, no matter how far up or down the ladder that company is, that you are lucky to be there.** Think of where you might be working and how few have the opportunity to share what you can share. Understand that every company gives you a chance to do what you love. Each performance is an opportunity for you to love others.

2. **Give your capital away for free from time to time.** If you let it, money can easily corrupt. Share it with those who are less fortunate. Don't tell anyone that you did it. If you tell anyone, you will be tempted to allow that attention to motivate you. This needs to be a secret. In addition, since your voice is part of your capital, sing from time to time in retirement villages or schools.

3. **Bring yummies to rehearsal for everyone to share.** It is a small gesture that others remember.

4. **Come to rehearsals ready with a plan to give in to the desires of your director and/or conductor.** Specifically yield, without argument, to one of their ideas that you disagree with. Remember, you are lucky to be there.

5. **Volunteer for a worthy non-profit organization that**

has nothing to do with opera. This could be your church, a Rotary Club, a homeless shelter or a Toys for Tots, for example. Connect with the world this way and understand how you are a part of it. Do not put this on your résumé.

6. **Help the next generation.** Get involved with spreading the gospel of music to children. Go to high schools and help the music students there understand how to do what you are doing. Meet freely with young people who want to interview you about what you do. Many of them are trying to decide if a career in the arts is worth it. Most of them have been told to stay away because "no one can make money in the arts." Help them catch a better vision than this.

7. **Talk to chorus members, tech people, prop people, stage managers, accompanists, costume designers, wig and makeup people, and ask them about their families and lives.** Find out their interests. If you have money, buy some of them thank-you gifts. Nothing is more thoughtful.

8. **If you have a car, offer to give rides to other singers.** Many singers are too afraid to ask, but could really use your help.

9. **Pray or meditate daily.** Spending time in introspection does a world of good for not only you, but everyone who has to work with you. In addition, this quiet, focused time will still your mind, calm your nerves, and give you perspective on why you do what you do.

10. **When you are praised by anyone, simply say "Thank you."** There are two wrong answers: the first is "Of course, I know" and the second is "No, I made a lot of mistakes." The first is clearly prideful; the second is not humble, but insulting to the person offering the compliment. Be grateful that your imperfect voice made

someone happy.

11. **When talking to others, obey the three sentence rule.** This means you need to learn to take turns. You speak three sentences, maximum, then they say as much as they want. If you embark on a discourse, you come across as a know-it-all, full of yourself and your ideas--someone who has nothing to learn from others.

12. **When talking to others, ninety percent of the time should be spent talking about them.** If they want to know about you and your life, they will ask. Do not offer information, nor slyly lead the conversation around to one of your accomplishments, no matter how much you want them to know what you've done. Ask them lots of questions. Get to know them. You have something to learn from everyone that you can apply to your own life.

13. **Thank people that do you favors**--even if they are being paid to do those favors for you. Show gratitude for everyone and everything around you.

14. **Thank people who criticize you, especially if it not their place to do so.** Remember, you are not thanking them for their intentions, but for the fact that you have been given an opportunity to grow.

15. **Apologize easily.** It is not a sign of weakness. Admit your flaws. If your behavior was public, admit it publicly, as quickly as you can. Don't be defensive when attacked.

16. **Find the person at rehearsals that seems to dislike you the most and be on the warpath to serve this person.** Don't worry if they never like you--there is no quid pro quo here. This is about changing your attitude, not theirs.

17. **Find something good to say about all your colleagues while you are singing at any opera company.** First, tell them each something that you like about them when you are alone with them, then, second,

compliment them in front of everyone else.

18. **Join a group that challenges your pride weekly.** If you are not into churches, then find something equivalent that will help you question your personality, remind you of death, renew perspective on your life, challenge your beliefs, and establish your ethical relationship to others.

19. **Constantly work on your weaknesses and personality flaws.** Remember, life is not about discovering "who you are" as much as it is about "changing who you are." Most of the time, desires, appetites and passions can change and be kept within certain boundaries. Seeking to improve your character on an ongoing basis is a sure fire way to keep you humble.

20. **Seek for the reasons you are alive, even if your questions lead to more questions.** There is nothing worse than people who think they have all of the answers and have nothing more to learn. Certainly, we can come to particular conclusions about life, from our limited perspectives, but keep in mind that all people see through a "glass darkly." The humble seem to be lucky enough to get the most answers.

Although the above is a list of actions, you will not be able to maintain them unless you can make them actual personality traits. This means that they must come from your heart; they must be manifestations of who you are.

It is not an accident the people envision opera singers as prideful, opulent, untouchable, and unapproachable. People seem to like them this way--it gives the audience something to talk about. The marketing of opera singers is partly to blame. However, this marketing doesn't accurately reflect the personalities of many of these performers. A few of the superstars, of necessity, must insulate or separate themselves for safety reasons after a certain level of fame. But the majority of singers who make a good living will tell you that diva-like behavior is not tolerated in the opera field. It destroys careers before they begin.

Some beginning singers, in an effort to emulate their favorite superstar, take on the characteristics of the diva, thinking it will bring them closer to a successful career. Others begin humbly, but begin to think too much of themselves as they begin to receive positive attention from admiring audiences.

In the long run, those who act most like divas not only end their careers prematurely, but end up spending the rest of their lives making other people miserable. Many become university professors who carry their cockiness down the halls of their scholarly institution. Others become coaches or private instructors, sinking their prideful claws into uninitiated young artists, ruining their chances for a career as well. Stay away from these people at all costs.

Shun pride in all its forms. It will not only hurt your career, but surround you with misery in the rest of your life. Replace it with a healthy understanding of your connection to others, and you will be on the path to becoming an authentic artist.

Chapter 8

The Personality of Growth

If at any time in your career you think you have arrived or that you can coast, think again. First, stagnation is almost impossible. You are either improving or deteriorating. Second, people can sense your devotion to your profession. If they think you are coasting with no real interest in improvement, they won't support you any more. Third, remember that the better you get, the more you will realize how bad you are. Knowledge increases with experience. Though you thought you would be happy once you arrived at a certain level, when you got there, you could see much further. You realized just how inadequate you are. The more you know, the more you discover you don't know.

Success in this field of high achievement requires a personality of growth. You need to be the kind of person that not only gets up when you fall, but one who looks for new ways to fail. You need to embrace all forms of risk-taking and falling on your face in front of others. But you also need to find ways that lead you toward the potential of falling even further. All growth requires risk.

Improvement demands that we leave our comfort zones. Once a habit is established, it no longer causes us pain. It enters the comfort zone. It is the development of a new habit that causes the greatest pain.

There are hundreds of habits that you need to develop just to get hired at an opera company. Each new habit requires focus and attention every day, and this may seem distracting.

Putting up with these distractions is part of the personality of growth. As soon as one habit is developed, you begin on the next habit. As a result, you never get to return to your comfort zone. This personality is rare in the world. It makes some people rich and it makes others great artists. Sometimes, it makes you both.

As someone who aspires to become an opera singer, you want to surround yourself with your profession. You become your environment. Because of this, you need to know how to create an atmosphere that will cause you to thrive in your career. Below is the 8-8-8 Formula for Artistic Nutrition (your "FAN" base) that will cultivate the kind of environment that will place you on a trajectory of growth. The three categories below will create an environment that immerses you in your profession, will give you an understanding of the world around you, and will offer a means to maintain a motivated mindset that keeps you moving forward.

Surrounding Yourself with Your Profession

If you put garbage in, you get garbage out. That is how our minds work. As you feed your brain with good things, especially things related to your career, you will begin to take on characteristics of those things--almost like osmosis. Your subconscious is operating all day, and you cannot afford to be unaware of your environment. Here are the eight ways that will most help you assimilate your profession:

1. **Listen to other opera singers.** Many musicians don't listen to music. Since they make it all day, they are happy to have a break from it. However, you cannot afford to do this, especially in the beginning. You are not listening to enjoy it, but to study it and become familiar with it. You need to recognize all of the famous voices of our time and the voices of the past. Listen to technique, interpretation, and intention. Know these singers by name. Take the best qualities of these performers and make them your own. Ask yourself why they inspire so many people. Do not do what so many insecure novices do, finding fault with these voices. You are listening to hear what these singers are doing right, not what they are doing wrong.

2. **Read books on vocal technique and pedagogy.** Even the best singer in the world doesn't sing perfectly. Even if you are getting jobs at large opera houses, you still need to continue to improve your technique. Keep pedagogical books on the bookshelf and read a bit as a supplement to your daily practice. Remember, the minute you think you have arrived, your career is over.

3. **Study music history.** Great artists are not simply singers. Musicians need to be well-rounded and understand the origins of music, how it evolved, and especially how it relates to the creation of their particular genre of music. Specifically, how did opera evolve and why? What were the influences? Who are the major operatic composers? You need to study their composition styles, understand the theory, and examine the form. The world rewards artists who do their

homework. Can you name the one hundred most performed operas, the roles involved, and recognize the arias? Adopt the habit of studying your profession.

4. **Study acting, go to plays, and watch movies.** Since opera is a hybrid art form, you are also an actor. This is usually the greatest weakness of most opera singers. Conversely, good acting will set you apart from the auditioning masses. When you watch a good movie or a go to a play, watch the eyes of the performers. The eyes will reflect the thoughts of the character, not simply the words coming out of their mouths. Notice the many things an actor must consider. Watch the motivation behind gestures and movement. Understand subtext and character development.

5. **Improve your non-singing skills.** Most great singers (not all, but most) are also good, if not great, pianists. They understand that their vocal line is not a melodic island unto itself, but part of a harmonic tapestry. Universities require piano skills from people studying voice or any instrument. It is the basic instrument of musicians. The better you get at the piano, the better you will be as a singer and an artist. Related to this is your understanding of harmony, and theory in particular. You need to understand Roman numeral analysis and a certain degree of ear training. You need to understand harmonic structure and get into the mind of the composers whose work you are presenting to the world. Try to compose your own music as part of this process of understanding the intentions of the composers whose works you perform. You also need to know how your vocal line fits into the opera. When you study and prepare an opera, you need to perceive what is going on in the orchestra pit. What kind of instruments are accompanying you and why? How does your understanding of the full score

affect your phrasing and interpretation? How does it affect your relationship with the conductor and his ability to create a cohesive picture? How does your singing affect the conductor's ability to lead the orchestra in after a *col canto* or recitative?

6. **Get involved with a local opera company.** Help your own community by supporting your local opera company if you have one--even if the company is smaller than those you generally sing with. Do what you can for them. Sing at their fundraisers, coach their singers if you are good enough, or sing with them if it is appropriate. You will not always be working, and in your time off, connect with people trying to create music in your own community. This is part of who you are.

7. **Teach.** You will learn more by teaching than any studying you do. Teaching others accesses a different part of your brain than that of being a student. It gives you not only more confidence, but puts you in the driver's seat. You will be amazed by the quality of the things you say when you are in teaching mode. You will also remind yourself, as you get back to the basics of singing, of things that are applicable to your own voice. You may feel that you are unqualified to teach. You are wrong. Every singer has something to offer. As you learn to explain concepts clearly to others, they become clearer to you as well. If you don't have piano skills, teaching will force you to get them. In addition, teaching is about passing on what you have learned to the next generation. If professionals don't teach, then that leaves all teaching to non-professionals--and what do they know? A lot less. Without the teaching by professionals, this art form would die. Your job is not to be the last opera singer alive, but to see that the art form continues and even improves, otherwise your career has been self-

indulgent.

8. **Befriend others in your profession who are goal-oriented.** Finally, you cannot and must not cut yourself off from others in your profession. You need to surround yourself with other professionals who are positive and growth-oriented. Many singers are negative and demoralized. They don't get jobs, and they act like victims. Stay away from these singers. They are poison to your motivation. Create a relationship with someone who will support your goals and whose goals you will support. Professional contacts are vital for your career. You need people with whom you can "talk shop" on a regular basis. You will all be growing in different ways, and your relationships will add to your own growth as you share the things you have learned from different perspectives.

Studying the World Around You

As an artist, you must understand that the ideas and information of the world affects your art. Your art is all about the world. It acts as both a reflection of society and also inspires people to change that society. How can an artist, through art, inspire change if that artist refuses to live in the real world and understands nothing about it? An artist must understand how civilizations evolve, what motivates human beings, and why people are willing to sacrifice for relationships, children, communities, and countries. Human beings and their interactions with others are what motivate the creation of your operas. In addition, you need practical skills and knowledge to function in the world. Here are the things you must do:

1. **Study history.** The first step you need to take to become a well-rounded human being is to understand the past. You can't understand your own life until you understand your environment and its origins. In addition, your operas are often historical. As part of your study of opera, you should understand the motivations of composers and librettists and the historical backgrounds of the characters you portray and interact with. History is the beginning of basic knowledge about people and their motivations. If you hated history in school, understand it was only the teacher who was boring. There are exciting ways to learn history through books and documentaries.

2. **Read biographies of important people.** Nothing is more inspiring than the lives of people who have achieved great things. If you want to do the same, study the minds and behavior of great people of the past and present. One of the ways that people learn to change their personalities is to surround themselves with the right personalities. If you can't become their friends directly, the next best thing is to read books about them. An autobiography can be even better. Then you get right into their minds, what drives them, and what makes them who they are.

3. **Be part of your community.** Live in the world you live in. If you are a traveling opera singer without a European fest contract, this is hard to do. However, you should have a home base somewhere. Arrange your life to be part of that community when you can. Support it in all its facets: political, social, and educational. Help that community thrive. Learn how others live in that community and understand the sacrifices they make to make those communities work. Part of learning how art makes people better is understanding what it means to be a normal person. What is normal? Most people are not

on the road most of the year. Most people form communities and relationships, and that is how society functions properly. Do your best to stay grounded.

4. **Cultivate relationships that are more important than your opera career.** As much as we believe in the arts, they are not the reason we are alive. Art is a tool that can help us understand ourselves in profound ways, but it is not the object of our existence, no matter what Tosca says. Even without opera, we would still be here, trying to discover what drives us or trying to create what drives us. Selfless relationships with others are what teach us the most about ourselves. How can we sing about human love to others when we have no idea what love really is? How can we portray sacrifice, when we are unwilling to make those sacrifices ourselves in even the smallest way? Opera plots are mostly about relationships, and yet, the opera world is filled with people who are involved in superficial relationships. In a way, this is why the European model of opera works better than the American model. American singers travel from opera house to opera house every month, developing relationships with people they will likely never see again. Instead of being with their families, they spend time staring at pictures of them backstage. In Europe, you can go home at night and experience a more well-rounded life that closely resembles the life most people live. For this reason, American opera singers have a reputation for being self-centered and paranoid. There are ways around this problem in America, but you must study it out and create a blueprint for the kind of life you want to live.

5. **Understand politics and economics.** Opera plots are often about political intrigues. Part of living in this world is understanding the various ways that humans have tried to create societies. The natures of those types of

organizations and governments create different results in happiness, standard of living, and the ability of humans to respond to problems. Some governments have been formed on the premise that man is basically good and can be trusted. Others believe that man's basic narcissistic nature requires a government that protects man from man. There have been many experiments throughout history. Governments rise and fall. An understanding of communism, socialism, fascism, democracy, pluralism, and theocracies, is basic to your comprehension of your place in society. Making sense of the economics behind these societies is more complicated, but it can help in your understanding of your opera career. For example, why is opera often "non-profit"? Why do some governments subsidize or even control the arts? Why do some countries not allow anything except religious singing? How does supply and demand affect the arts? If you want to survive as an artist, you may need money. If so, you need to understand what drives economics. You need to understand the difference between wage/labor capitalism and product/service capitalism. You need to perceive the difference between working for yourself and working for someone else. You need to learn how artists were affected when they moved from being supported servants of the aristocracy to being self-sufficient. Money will affect you and the artistic decisions you make.

6. **Understand world religions.** Nothing motivates and moves the world more than religion. Politics and government don't come close to affecting society as much as the deep-seated belief systems that dominate various regions of the world. Governments can restrict and control the behavior of man, but religion controls the heart of man. In the long run, people's hearts dictate

their behavior. Many people today claim to not be "religious" or "churchgoing," but this is irrelevant. Cultures at their core have a religious heritage. Wars around the world are fought for religious reasons. The plots of the operas that you sing are often about religious conflicts. The politics of your area are often driven by religious ideas. No one can be a citizen of this world without understanding the major world religions and the dominant religions of the area in which they live. Whether you ascribe to any of the beliefs of these religions or not, you should learn the perspectives of these belief systems. When you do, you should learn them directly from the people that follow them. Unfortunately, the world is full of instruction about world religions from biased perspectives. In the war of ideas, people naturally try to demonize, dehumanize, and inaccurately represent people whose ideology is different from theirs. Get your information from the source.

7. **Study science, technology, math, and psychology.** You live in a world that is now controlled by and obsessed with science and technology. You need computer and internet skills to function in today's society, especially if you want to maintain an opera career. In addition, you need math skills to understand the complexities of managing your opera business. You need more than the ability to balance and reconcile a checkbook; you need to understand investment, compound interest, and tax deductions. In addition to money, you need to understand the mind. Understanding the principles of psychology will help you greatly in your career. Learning to use logical and rational thought can help you in making business decisions and interacting with others. It will help you with your own motivations as well as the motivations of the characters you play on

stage.

8. **Read the classics.** An artist should be well-read. Literature is one of the foundations of opera. Librettos and other kinds of literature are also works of art. Words are the beginning and the end of opera. The music should be there to serve the libretto, not the other way around. In addition, you will be interacting with many people in your career, many of whom are well-educated and wealthy. Familiarity with literature is required in these interactions. People quote and use idiomatic expressions from literature on a regular basis. Your ignorance will be difficult to hide forever and may keep you from opportunities to advance in your career. You are part of the world you live in and need to understand that world if you wish to effectively shape it through art.

Staying Motivated

No one is self-motivated. It may seem as if some people are, but when you ask them, there is almost always someone who motivates them as well. In addition, motivation has a short shelf life. You can be inspired to do something great with your life one day, and, three days later, be back sitting on your sofa watching television until the late hours of the night, wondering what is wrong with you. Motivation is vision, and it can't be found in a pill. Like all relationships, it must be nurtured. Here is how to get started:

1. **Set Goals.** When you do this, begin with the end in mind. Too many people set goals backwards. They begin with their daily goals. As discussed in chapter one, pilots file a flight plan before they take off and know their destination. When headwinds come, they make

adjustments and continue their journey. Likewise, you need to start with your destination in mind and work backwards. Design your life by creating your ultimate goals, then figure out where you would be just before you reach those goals. Then, determine where you might be just before that. Continue in this fashion until you have set monthly, weekly and finally, daily objectives. People are afraid of writing goals down. But they must be written, or they are only wishes. Writing your plan commits you to a course of action. People often don't like to write down their goals so that they have an "out" if they fail. They can say, "I didn't really want to do that anyway." If it wasn't written down, they didn't fail because it wasn't real. You need to be willing to put it on the line. Write your goals down; review them regularly. Buy books on goal setting. Try different methods. Write them on your mirror. Speak them out loud every day. Apply them. You cannot get what you want without a plan.

2. **Read motivational books and listen to motivational tapes.** We need others to stay motivated. In addition to reading biographies, listen to people who professionally search for motivational stories and ideas and share them with the public in inspiring ways. Some call this pop-psychology, as if to denigrate it in some way. Certainly, some of it is fluffy, but motivation isn't always about intellect. Emotions are not always friends to the intellect. Straight psychology is important, but motivational psychology is also a bedrock of achievement. If one is to change long-standing habits and create new ones, desire must be cultivated. Play these self-improvement CDs in your car when you drive anywhere or when you ride the bus or train. Put them on your iPod and listen every time you get a spare moment.

3. **Go to motivational events.** Some people would put church, synagogue, or other places of worship in this category. There is a reason people go to these places every week. People need regular doses of motivation. In addition to writing books and creating recordings, PMA (Positive Mental Attitude) speakers travel regularly and are great sources of motivation and inspiration for life. Wayne Dyer, Tony Robbins, Zig Ziglar, Dale Carnegie, Jim Rohn, and many others are or were known for their ability to inspire people in large groups, conferences or seminars. Many of them still hold multi-day seminars that you can attend, or they sell workbooks and recordings that you can purchase. They are well worth the investment. They are all very different in their approaches, sense of humor, and perspectives on life. You will have to find the personality that fits you best. All have the ability to motivate well.

4. **Find motivational friends.** You must associate with friends who are positive in their outlooks on life. Though you may feel more powerful making friends with lots of problems to solve, or feel as if you are doing a great service by rescuing people on a regular basis, this approach will leave you with little energy to spare. You cannot spend time with a pessimist without becoming negative yourself. We all only have time for so many friends in our lives. Choose friends who have goals, who are positive and upbeat, and who support your goals. In a true friendship, you build each other up. It cannot be a one-way street.

5. **Turn off corporate sponsored news.** It is poison. In America, people like to speak of a free press, but it is not anything of the sort. Money drives the news as long as there are commercials or corporate sponsors. While news organizations are beholden to corporate interests,

then they will broadcast what people want to hear and see. If these corporations can keep you on their stations, you watch their commercials. To keep you there, they need to feed you a steady diet of the sensational and the extreme. You will read in the papers about murders, rapes, death, tornados, hurricanes, robberies and other salacious material, and the stories of the simple goodness of people will be relegated to a back page. Do we really care which famous superstars wore or misplaced their underwear when leaving a limo? You will only reap negativity from most corporate news. Get your news from other sources, including non-corporate sponsored internet sites or PBS, for example. Corporate news will paint a picture of despair and cause you to lose faith in other humans. It will also support any negative personality traits you may already have.

6. **Stop saying negative things out loud or in your head.** You are what you think and say. The dramas you allow to play out on the stage of your mind every day determine who you become. You train yourself, subconsciously, to behave in ways that correspond to your dominant thoughts. If they are thoughts of fear, you will attract those fears. If they are thoughts of joy, you will attract those joys. Positive affirmations, read aloud daily, work well because they program the filters of your brain to accept, hear, and be aware of that which you most desire. Remember, when it comes to your thoughts, your brain doesn't know the difference between what you want and what you don't want. It only records what you think about, and then goes into subconscious overdrive to bring you the fruits of those thoughts. You cannot risk pessimistic indulgences. Don't speak negatively about anything and don't think you can avoid the negative consequences of saying things only in your mind.

Everything you say and do, both in reality and in the imaginations of your heart, programs your life.

7. **Reverse negative comments by others.** When someone around you says something negative, counter it with something positive. If a butterfly can flap its wings and cause a hurricane on the other side of the globe, then a negative or positive idea, expressed out loud can circumnavigate the world and change millions of lives. There are no idle comments. Words have power.

8. **Exercise and eat right.** You can't love others until you learn to love yourself first. But that's not the only reason to take care of yourself. First, depression and obesity have been linked for years--and it's not because you are depressed that you are fat. Exercise and proper nutrition help your body function correctly. Blood flow to your brain is increased through exercise. Chemicals that induce optimism and that help you solve problems are spread throughout your body. Secondly, in today's society, healthy opera singers get more jobs. Remember, you are competing against great singers who don't have health or weight issues. Finally, singers who are not fit have a tendency to get sick more often than those that are not. Sickness is anathema to an opera career. Singers who get sick get negative reputations, and they don't get jobs. For so many reasons, get healthy.

This 8-8-8 Formula for Artistic Nutrition will change most lives in a dramatic way. It may be uncomfortable for you. But growth is always uncomfortable. The reward for that lack of comfort is profound. The tasks in this formula will help develop those aspects of your personality you will need to have a truly successful artistic life. If you have made it this far in this book and haven't given up yet, you may be ready to begin living this life.

Chapter 9

Living an Artistic Life

The life of an artist is filled with both sorrow and indescribable joy. It is unusual, often strange, both organized and unorganized. Living the life of an artist includes translating the abstract into the ordered and back again on a daily basis. It involves expressing life as a relationship of both the left and right hemispheres of the brain. In addition, it also means spending your life with the symbolic and learning to communicate beyond language. Understanding and communicating in non-discursive thought (thoughts without words) is a foundational practice of the artist.

Wonderful arts philosophers have written books on this subject. They also describe the reasons that the arts are necessary to an advancing society while expounding on the meaning of the arts to us in our lives. One of the best arts philosophers is Dr. Susanne Langer. Many of Ms. Langer's books are used as basic textbooks in many universities. Some of her books are more accessible than others, so you might begin with the compilation of some of her short lectures in *Problems of Art: Ten Philosophical Lectures (1957)*. If you want something more difficult and more profound, read *Feeling and Form: A Theory of Art (1953)* or her first major work, *Philosophy in a New Key (1942)*. This book expounded upon ideas that have become common today in philosophy: that there is a basic and pervasive human need to symbolize, to invent meanings, and to invest meanings in one's world. This is advanced reading, usually reserved for university classrooms, but the journey is well worth the effort. You might say that you are a singer and not a philosopher, but that is not true. The more you understand the reasons you do what you do, the better you will be as a performer and an artist. Don't shy away from the difficult because you believe that the easy will bring you the same rewards.

Believe What you do is Valuable

An artistic career will not last if you don't believe that what you do is necessary. You will be surrounded by people who think that the arts are an indulgence or simply an extra-curricular activity. Rarely does an artist achieve greatness in his or her profession without coming up against these kinds of negative influences. People will tell you that the joy that you feel in the creation of art is something that human beings are not supposed to experience. "Get a real job" is the mantra of the masses. So you get a "real" job, spend your life pushing pencils, balancing books, answering phones, and then you die. What was it all for? Doing something worthwhile doesn't require misery. Misery does, however, sometimes love company.

Your mantra to these people should be, "...and then you die." What is the point? Live a life that adds something to the world. The arts do that. They are fundamental to a evolving society. As an artist, you need to know how to defend, proclaim, and preach the arts to others. Don't be caught without answers to the dream-crushing drivel that ruins the life of children everywhere. The next time people try to cut arts from a school budget or curriculum, march into the school board meeting and tell its members in no uncertain terms why the arts are more important than reading, writing, and arithmetic.

If you don't have the courage to do this vocally, do you really believe it internally? If you cannot justify what you do in your own mind, then you will not be able to have the stamina or perseverance to do what it takes to be a great artist. Too many artists stammer and stutter when confronted by these society-killers. This is one reason why a philosophy of the arts must be studied.

We live in a society that rewards people who bring trash to the market place. We reward those in the business of beating each other up. We reward the inventor of the "Pet Rock." Each generation brings a new, lower level of inanity to this market place, appealing to our basest instincts. The biggest money maker on the internet is pornography. This was not always the case, but people are often seduced by the easy, the route that requires no thought, no introspection, and no deliberation. Too many people wish that they could have something for nothing. Singers often want careers without putting in the work. People want to learn the piano in "ten easy lessons."

Society is built on the backs of the creative. However, the creative problem-solving part of the brain is underdeveloped by schools. Instead, schools focus on serving businesses and corporations throughout a child's education and end by plugging the matriculated into a corporate machine upon graduation. Most people learn to do, and they don't learn how to create. Where are the Einsteins and the Edisons? Do we teach people to use or fix computers rather than be the inventor of the computer?

The arts develop the problem-solving side of the brain. They inspire our greatest inventors and leaders (as opposed to managers). They raise IQ scores across the board. They raise math and language scores. They inspire people to be better. They give people a reason to live.

People would not spend so much money on music if it were worthless. Nearly everyone has some kind of MP3 player or iPod. In spite of the fact that people often choose the lowest forms of art in the market place, people also respond to challenges. When we offer something profound to people, they will often step up and try understand it. At least the leaders of society will respond--and that is who you are trying to reach.

You don't need to reach everyone with your art. Pavarotti did a great job of marketing to the masses and opening their eyes to a new art form. In Europe, the famous "Three Tenor" concert video topped even the pop charts. This means there are a lot of people, more than we may think, that are willing to be influenced by higher art.

When we present an artistic offering to an audience, we prompt feelings that are not easily explained. In order to communicate this non-discursive expression to others, we often try to make it discursive. As we engage in this process, we find we have to create new words. This improves our ability to communicate and expands our language. Language helps society grow, and the arts inspire and improve language.

It is not the purpose of this book to defend these ideas, but to inspire you to pick up an arts philosophy book and study these concepts for yourself. Learn to understand the importance of what you do in a thriving society. Learn to defend it to yourself and others.

Supporting Beauty

Many artists in the world have dedicated their lives to their fields of art. Each artist has something unique to offer. Each artist has a special perspective through which they interpret the world. You can learn something from each of them.

Many artists understand their business, know how to network and market, and know how to run the business side of their profession. But, unfortunately, many talented people are weak in this. Most artists do not have a patron who will support their profession so they can only focus on their art. So many of these great artists fall by the wayside, their music unheard, their paintings unseen, or their literature unread.

Because you understand the need for art in this world, you, as an artist yourself, should support the arts and artists of all kinds. There are many ways to help them. If you have money, you can donate. You can also donate your time or your own talent as a way to fund them. If you are a good businessperson, teach them your secrets.

Seek out art worthy of support. Go to art shows and galleries. Stroll down sidewalks where impecunious artists are selling their works. You will often find art in unlikely places. Go to off-Broadway shows rather than Broadway shows. See lesser-known acting troupes perform. Attend the performances of small opera companies or small theater companies. Go to arts towns and browse the shops. Although kitsch exists out there, and you may encounter more poor singers than good ones, you will also find many gems.

Buy good art and put it up in your house. Listen to new composers and buy their music. If it is good, convince someone to perform it. Have informal concerts in your home. Go to a poetry reading. Befriend other artists. Exchange ideas. Support the goals of others. Encourage them and attend their concerts and showings.

Create beauty yourself in all you do. Many people try to separate their artistic career from their "normal life." There should be no difference. You cannot separate the two and should not try. Your life is a poem. It is a drama that is playing out both in the physical world and in your mind. You are the dramaturge of your own life which is being expressed at every minute. You can create a life of beauty and joy, a life of poetry and profundity, or you can fill your life with the mundane and then live to be on the stage.

Unfortunately, too many artists live on this roller coaster. They live for the performance and despise the details of the other aspects of their life. However, this teeter-totter way of living doesn't bring peace. It negates the art these artists create. You cannot get up on stage and sing about the beauty of life, trying to inspire people to live, and secretly hate the very life you are portraying. It makes you not only a liar, but a transparent one.

What is your goal as an artist? What do see when you look at the world? You can notice the amazing beauty around you, or you can choose see the gutters and sewer systems of humanity. If you are to create beauty, you need to seek beauty. This is more than a simple "glass half empty" versus "glass half full" mentality. This is a glass overflowing with joy and purpose.

Many artists attempt to portray the degradation of man. This can fail abysmally if there is no contrast in the work. All art requires antagonism, but if artists, depressed about the world and their lives, focus on the horrors of the world, attempting to rip hope from their audiences, then they are using their artistic skills destructively. Equally, if an artist, afraid to depict the dark sides of life at all, tries to depict only goodness, that artist will equally fail. Light without darkness is not light at all and vice versa. As opposites, they give each other their meaning. This is why good art is always about contrast.

Artists need to be aware of what the world needs. It doesn't need more evil. It needs more sensitivity, not less. It doesn't need additional violence and lust. It is easy to press the buttons of your audience by appealing to their baser instincts; but it is hard to fill their hearts with penetrating perceptions and inspirational ideas.

Beauty is more difficult to create than decay. Good artists need to be more sensitive than other people, not less. Beauty is found through sensitivity and peace. The noise of the world can dampen our ability to find and understand that peace. But you must believe that it is everywhere, waiting to be found.

Artists are often accused of seeing the world through rose-colored glasses. But the truth is that most people see the world through mud-covered glasses. It is your privilege as an artist to see beauty where others do not and bring that beauty to the attention of others.

Finding and supporting beauty is not intended to negate the fact that pain exists. It does. But people can respond to pain differently. We are surrounded by negativity at every turn. Victims abound. Pain is part of the process of life, but we can find great joy, even amidst that pain.

Finding Joy in Pain

Without sorrow, there is no joy. Without pain, there is no pleasure. There is indeed opposition in all things. People cannot live lives that are painless. We can put up psychological barriers to try to keep ourselves from getting hurt, but in doing this we simultaneously cut ourselves off from any chance of happiness.

Pain will always be in our lives. We either inflict it upon ourselves, or life inflicts it upon us. For example, we can go through the pain of exercise, or we can endure the pains and health hazards associated with being out of shape. Either way, we have to endure pain. We might as well inflict it upon ourselves by choice rather than whining or complaining about how horrible the world is to have consequences for our laziness.

Everyone has the same twenty-four hours in a day. You can choose your pain. You can go through the pain of changing your personality as described in this book, or you can experience the pain of working solely for money. You may later say to yourself, "What if I had changed my daily habits back when I had a chance?" You can live with the pain of "what ifs" for the rest of your life. That is your choice.

Since pain is inevitable, what matters is how we respond to it when it comes our way. Pain can cause our characters to grow. It can make us strong, or we can allow it to crush us. Artists embrace pain because it feeds their art. It inspires composers, painters, and authors. It demonstrates contrast and opposition. Opera is one response to pain. It tells stories of pain and how different people respond to it.

Each trial we endure offers us something to learn and a way to grow. The stronger we get, the more joy we can experience. Gratitude stems from pain. We are more grateful after the pain has passed than we would have been had it never come. Appetite control makes food taste better. Captivity makes freedom sweet.

The heart of an artist must be filled with both painful and joyful experiences. The personality of an artist is never shut off from psychological pain. If you put up protective barriers, you will never be able to get up on stage and throw yourself on the mercy of an audience emotionally, intellectually, or otherwise.

Let go now of your need to avoid pain now. Be willing to love with no strings attached. Give your gift freely. Love your audience. Love those that judge you at auditions, competitions, or the breakfast table. All people want love. Give it to them.

Remember, it's okay when people reject your gift. Your joy

comes from the giving of love, whether or not your audience accepts that gift. When your heart is filled with love, you can endure even the greatest pains. Your yoke will be easy, and your burden will be light.

Chapter 10

There is no Competition

With all the lifestyle and personality changes described in this book, you may be feeling overwhelmed. You can choose what to do with this information. You can get depressed and go get a job at Walmart. You can watch the television every night until you fall asleep on the couch. You can sit on trains, buses and subways and stare straight ahead as you fritter away precious time to learn new skills. You can play the lottery. Or you can begin this adventure with the resolve to change a single habit in your life. You can write down your goals and turn them into a reality.

It's fine to be overwhelmed. When people look at the big picture and see all of the changes that they will have to make to become the person they want to become, they may feel as if they are drinking from a fire hydrant. You are now drowning in information. Don't freak out. No one becomes anything great overnight. You aren't expected to either. Relax.

There will always be room for people to move into the arts. There isn't a limited amount of space, and there isn't a limited amount of time. There is no hurry. Singers who are in a rush are the ones who fail. This isn't about reaching a destination, but rather about the journey. It's about what you are becoming, not what you are achieving. You are becoming an artist, not simply acting like one. If you only try to force yourself into the behaviors of this book, you will burn out and eventually quit. You cannot maintain this kind of activity without a change of heart--a fundamental change in who you are. That kind of change takes time--a lot of it.

The Behavior of Those in the Middle.

Most singers never make it to the top of their profession. Most singers never find a way to make a living as a singer. Many of them had been told that if they go to college and do their homework, upon graduation, they will be handed a job. Many of them have spent eight hard years in college and feel that they deserve jobs after all this work. Other professions seem to work that way. College students in computer science can often expect head hunters to come to their college, looking to hire graduates. If you study medicine, you know exactly what hoops you must jump through before you can practice medicine. If you want to be a lawyer, you take a test, and voilà, you are a lawyer.

It would be great if you could take a test and, suddenly, you are a paid opera singer. Sadly, this isn't the case. Not only will opera singers' incomes arrive from thousands of different sources throughout their lives, but they will need to spend much of their lives auditioning for new jobs. When a college student graduates, he or she is rarely ready for a professional career.

One of the principal reasons for this is that these young singers do not possess the personality requirements outlined in this book. Many are in the mindset of the doctor and the lawyer going to school, and think all their study ought to be finished so they can move on with their lives.

Singers may hear stories in college about all the competition there is in the opera field. However, competition doesn't exist at the top. It only exists in the middle. Many singers may become good performers in college. Unfortunately, that just makes Granny want to hire you to sing at her funeral. It is not enough to be a good singer, you need to be a great one.

Singers in the middle levels of the profession have certain traits that separate them from great artists:

1. **They don't focus on what they need to fix in their technique.** Instead, they sing through songs and indulge in the enjoyment of their own voices. They don't realize that they could progress ten times faster by practicing only what they cannot do, rather than what they can. They see technique and scale work as boring, so they spend their time with the vocal literature instead.

2. **They think they have arrived.** Because people around them offer effusive approbation on a regular basis, they don't feel the need to get any better. After they get a few opera contracts, they think they are significantly better than they really are and stop working on their vocal technique.

3. **They think a college degree means something.** They put their degrees on their respective walls at home. They care more about the degree than the information and instruction that they had the opportunity to get in college. They were the ones who said, "Will this be on the test?" They were never willing to sacrifice a grade in school to spend more time learning what they needed to learn for their career. They mistakenly believed that the curriculum designed for them at college was sufficient for

what they needed to be an opera singer. They believe that college was the only necessary bridge between high school and a professional career.

4. **They're happy just being good.** They are not motivated to be great. They don't have the drive to perfect themselves. They are fine with little periodic mistakes. Sometimes they think that people won't notice a mispronounced word here or a missed dotted rhythm there. They ignore details on the page written by the composer and only think about the notes. They get to the top of the totem pole wherever they are singing and stay there, basking in the admiration of others rather than moving on to a new location where they are at the bottom of a new totem pole.

5. **They don't see personality as a foundational element of their success.** They try to improve technique, learn about the business, and make connections, but they keep finding themselves getting in the way of their own success. They still have stage fright, they still think that an opera career is about luck, they still think that they can act any way that they want, and their voice will carry them through. They are rarely committed enough to their craft to add anything to the art form. They may have diva problems or issues with self-esteem. Or they are just plain lazy.

6. **They only get their information from one source.** They attach themselves to one teacher or one coach and put all their trust in that opinion. They don't understand that no single person has all the answers, and that most singers require multiple sources of information to make sense of a career. In a misguided desire to be nice, they often don't have the guts to stop studying or coaching with someone and move on. Many of these types of singers are conflict-avoiders. Or they are too trusting or

too fearful of the unknown.

7. **They have trouble with criticism.** They run from all correction. When a director or a conductor criticizes, they visibly freeze up, or they argue and defend themselves. They often believe that after all the work and study they have put into preparing a role, theirs is the only way to interpret the score. They may have other emotional hang-ups and have put up a wall to criticism. They offend other artists, directors, conductors, and designers they work with because listening to the opinions of others would mean admitting that their own opinion might be wrong.

8. **They learn a little, but not enough.** They learn a little piano, but not enough to be a musician. They study the required one semester of a language in school, but have no desire to develop fluency. They do the minimum, thinking that it will be enough. They rarely study acting, hoping that it is enough to merely understand stage right and stage left. They don't bother studying performance practice, interpretation, conducting, audition techniques, IPA symbols, coloratura technique, or formal analysis.

9. **They waste time.** They wait for buses, they wait in lines, and they sit in offices in mindless dazes. They don't carry language cards or pedagogical books to use while they are waiting. They watch too much television, go to too many parties, or spend too much time on the internet, not realizing that they are burning away hours of their lives that they will never get back. They don't realize that everyone has the same twenty-four hours in a day, and they blame their lack of success on a lack of time. Sometimes, these people actually work hard, but they confuse activity with accomplishment. They don't focus precious practice time working on the hard things. Instead, they waste time in meaningless repetitive actions

that lead nowhere.

10. **They don't read books like this.** They don't seek change. Information outside their sphere of awareness doesn't exist. So, they avoid books on behavioral change or personal awareness. Introspection is too painful.

11. **They don't know how to treat their art as a business.** They may be good artists, but don't know how to bring it to the masses. They don't know how to balance a checkbook, do their taxes, or invest their money. They don't know how to create a résumé or get an agent. And if they figure out how to get an agent, they don't understand the relationship. They don't understand that the first priority of an opera singer who has a job is to get hired again.

12. **They don't set and write down goals.** They don't want to commit themselves and then fail at the top of their voices. They don't clearly state, in writing, what it is that they want, and then create a plan to get there. Instead, they wander around the base of Mount Everest and hope that they will magically end up on top. They believe that a strong desire is enough. They can see no clear path to their dreams because they haven't created that path.

13. **They look for what is wrong with famous singers instead of focusing on what they do right.** They have honed their critical skills in college and spend their time tearing apart the success of others. They are usually secretly (and not so secretly) jealous of other singers who win competitions or get jobs that they do not. They can't find a way to be happy for others. But beyond that, they cannot look at famous singers and ask themselves what positive things those singers have done that have added to their success. They often spend much of their time berating themselves for all their weaknesses and mistakes,

rather than learning from those mistakes and moving on.

14. **They are afraid of marketing and networking.** They don't want to sell themselves. They would rather hide in a cubicle practicing all day than make friends and business acquaintances. They are embarrassed or ashamed to ask others for help. They feel that marketing is a kind of prostitution, instead of a way to let people know that you have a product or service available. They don't realize that no one can hire opera singers if they remain invisible. They also are fairly self-centered and don't think of their relationships as inter-dependent, but rather see relationships as something there to serve them. They don't immediately see how they might be able to help someone else achieve their goals as well.

15. **They believe all kinds of erroneous things about their chances to make it in the business.** They believe in luck and chance, as if success in an opera career were a crap shoot. They believe that singers get jobs because of who they sleep with, or who was in the right place at the right time. They believe that there just aren't that many jobs out there. They don't take responsibility for their own lives and are unable to accept that they are where they are because of decisions that they have made up to this point. They believe that life is cruel.

16. **They put out negative energy.** They come across as desperate during auditions or act as if they are too good for the opera companies that want to offer them jobs. They broadcast their feelings about their colleagues, and because artists pick up on subtle emotions for a living, their colleagues may exaggerate these impressions and imagine the worst.

17. **They have too many things they like to do.** Their focus is split. They may be talented individuals in many areas, but they focus on too many of these areas at once,

becoming good at all of them, but not great at any of them. They don't understand that being a great artist will require them to choose, at least for a time. They may love to play sports, work out for hours a day, or make violins. Whatever their hobbies, they get distracted by filling their lives up with too many wonderful things. People can do anything, but they can't do everything.

18. **They don't feel worthy of success.** Their belief creates their own reality. They literally cut themselves off from opportunities that they might have because their subconscious filters out what does not correspond to their low self-images. They don't realize that thoughts are things. They think the universe is out to get them, and rightly so.

19. **They create something to "fall back on."** They don't realize that creating something to fall back on means that they will fall back on that thing. They get advanced degrees in education or other disciplines "just in case" that opera career doesn't work out. They are afraid to go out without the safety net. Most of these people live their lives governed by fear, with all kinds of safety nets in place. They will attract their fears every time. They don't live with the imperative to be an artist. They don't understand that great artists know in their hearts that this is what they have to do for a living, and they make it happen.

Why You Can and Should Be an Artist

Is becoming an artist a blessing only afforded a select few? Is it only possible for the very talented to make it? No, and no again. If you want it, you can have it. Many singers get upset if success doesn't seem to be coming their way. They don't understand what is wrong. Most often it is not a lack of desire, but rather a personality problem.

Many singers don't want to hear this. In general, people don't want to hear that their success, in large part, is temperament-based and not skill-based. Skills can't develop properly if there is a personality issue.

Every artist is different, and this book doesn't cover the dispositions of all artists. But it does give a good general overview of the personality type required to be successful in the arts. There are always exceptions, and you can spend your time trying to find them. But that won't serve you or your career. People like to be exceptions, so they can avoid the discipline required by rules. However, true exceptions are only revealed to those who learn and understand the rules first.

But the serious question is whether or not you should move ahead on this bold enterprise. You should, absolutely. It may seem a daunting task to make all these changes in your life or to change your entire perspective on the universe. You may be far away from having the mindset, habits, and doggedness described in this book. But deep down, you know you are on this earth to create. You not only appreciate beauty, but you have a song you need to sing. You may not yet have the skill to bring it out in the way you would like, but that is just a matter of time. Time is something everyone has been given equally, and then we all die. And what was the point of our lives?

It was not to worry about paying our bills, so that we could send our kids to college and hope they could grow up to worry about paying their bills. We are here to find joy, not worry. We have too few musicians--real artists--out in the world. However, there are a lot of singers out there.

Remember, there is a lot of room at the top, but no room in the middle. If you go for the big goal, you will find no competition. An amazing few do what is necessary to become great artists. However, it is the artists of the world who shape the future. It is the artists who teach our children how to use their creative minds. By awakening the problem-solving parts of the mind, we inspire solutions to the world's dilemmas. It is the artists who bring us hope and reveal a vision of what we can become, both individually and as a society.

When people walk out of a production or a gallery, they are inspired to be better. They walk out in awe of human potential. It is that spark of vision that propels innovation and productivity. It inspires people to keep their own goals, to follow their dreams, and to improve their relationships. Music, in particular, digs deep into the soul and carves out new human beings. It can elevate perceptions and exalt understanding beyond language. In the right hands, it can change the world in a way that is beyond the reach of the most eloquent diplomacy.

There are not enough artists. There are many hobbyists and entertainers. You are not an entertainer; you are an artist. Being an artist is not only one of the most noble things you can choose to do with your life, but it is a vital part of everyone's life.

Do not allow your family, your friends, your colleagues, your teachers, your shrink, your newspapers, your clergyman, or anyone else tell you not to live your life as an artist. If they chose not to do it, that was their choice and their life. Do not even allow this book to deter you from choosing this path. Life is hard whether or not you choose to follow the outlines of this book. Don't run away from hard work. Art must be a struggle for both the body and the mind. There will be pain and difficulty along the way, but it will be worth it. It is not meant to be easy; it is meant to be beautiful. It will bring you and others indescribable joy.

Remember, as a synthesis of almost all of the artistic fields, opera may be the most difficult and audacious enterprise. It represents the disciplines of music, dance, the visual arts, the language and literature arts, and the dramatic arts. An opera singer is expected to be great at most of these. People feel fortunate if they attend an opera and are moved by all of the performers because finding good operatic performers is difficult. This is why there is so much room for people who pull it all together. There is room for you.

Of all of the negative people who will try to dissuade you from entering the arts, you may be your worst enemy. Do not allow your personality to get in the way of doing what needs to be done. Do not sabotage the opportunities that are waiting for you because you are filled with negative self-talk and other forms of mental self-abuse. You can change if you need to. Develop new habits of thinking, new habits of practicing, new habits of living, and new habits of learning until you can do them in your sleep. Don't be afraid. Let the world hear the song you've been waiting to sing.

To keep up with Dan Montez, his writing, lectures, private and public coaching, performances, and books visit:

http://danmontez.com

For information about his non-profit opera company, *Taconic Opera*, their performance schedule, and opportunities to support, visit them at:

http://taconicopera.org

Also visit the company on *Facebook* and *Twitter*.

Made in the USA
Charleston, SC
08 May 2011